IN NEED OF LOVE

ANXIETY, DEPRESSION, AND MY PERSONAL BATTLE FOR A LIFE WITH MEANING

ALEX FISCHLER

published by

duffin creative

los angeles

Published in the USA by
Duffin Creative
11684 Ventura Blvd #205
Studio City, CA 91604
Visit us on the Web at duffincreative.com

ISBN-10: 061587259X
ISBN-13: 978-0615872599

First Edition
Printed in the United States of America

This book is dedicated to my father.

TABLE OF CONTENTS

PREFACE
by Brenda Lee

THIS IS A BOOK THAT TAKES PAINS TO EXPRESS THE TRUTH OF what happened. It documents a boy's life where "truths" only came out in glimpses: first through a child's unwitting observations of his family, but then through a young adult's questioning view of—well—*everything*. The narrator struggles to sort through all the confusion, the disturbances that erupted at home, the episodes between loved ones that brought about further chaos—all in an effort to form a more complete and honest picture of his world. But no matter how much he tries to understand it, no matter how hard he fights for answers to fill in the gaps, he's never far from feelings of rage, fear, guilt, and disappointment.

Is this a coming-of-age story? Maybe. Will these chapters turn the Oedipal son theory on its head? No doubt. All I know is that it is Alex's catharsis—years in the making—after he took the first, biggest step of his adult life and left his mother's house in the summer of 2010.

As a former high school teacher, I believe this is not your typical teenager rebelling against authority. In many ways Alex does fit the mold of today's youth—a survivor of his parents' divorce, settling somewhat into two separate households with and without stepsiblings, longing for freedom but recognizing the reality. No, what sets Alex's story apart from others—what he clearly longs to make sense of in this book—is how those early glimpses of the truth were symptoms of his parents' failed relationship and, by turns, symptoms of the slow, agonizing breakdown of his own relationship with his mother.

Much to his credit and through regular therapy, Alex found ways to cope during his teen years, Sports, music, and writing it down all helped. Luckily, he did not succumb to hard drugs or violence. I have gotten to know Alex these last five years and am one of dozens rooting for him to come to terms with it all. He's determined to, certainly smart enough to, and resourceful beyond a single parent's wildest dreams. If completing this book allows Alex to finally move on and, in the process, should its raw detailing of emotional and verbal abuse, of love meted out conditionally and for appearance's sake—should any of it resonate with other young people, how important—how honest—is that?

Alex is my stepson—not officially yet, but soon! I am proud of his determination to resolve the past which, every good therapist knows, will continue to inform his future. I am impressed with his deep loyalty to us, his family and friends, even as we all continue to bump up against our own weaknesses and limitations. I admire most the relationship Alex has with his father with whom he shares every thought and feeling, no holds barred, and whose unwavering love paves the way to one boy growing into a force of a man.

Brenda Lee
July 2013

FOREWORD
by Steven Karr

Dear Alex,

During the past five years I have realized that you are the strongest fighter I have ever met. I don't know if I could deal with anything that you have had to deal with in your life. You have admirably battled through all of it. I think the best part of all is that you use your past experiences as fuel to create a better life and set goals. I also think you have made me a better person and friend.

When you were suicidal I was worried. I didn't want to think of what life would be like without you. I know there were a lot of times where you could have thrown in the towel. But somehow you had it within yourself to keep going. That fight in you has kept your life together and you have a very bright future.

I know I cannot relate to most of your home life or most of your experience. But I have always tried to be there and to listen to you and help you along the way. Seeing what you have gone through has made me appreciate my life and to respect the person you are. Most important, it has strengthened our friendship.

I have seen clear growth in the five years I have known you. During sophomore year in high school you were a quiet guy who enjoyed talking sports. Throughout junior year you dealt with shitty relationships with girls, which took their toll on you. By senior year you were in a living hell.

The worst thing I have experienced in my life was seeing you at your lowest point. You were miserable, even during the good times. You were not really present because of depression, anxiety and pills.

You have grown up a lot faster than you wanted to. I think you are a forty-year-old in a twenty-year-old's body. In reality that is the only choice you had. Honestly, you wouldn't be alive now if you didn't grow up as quickly as you did.

Once you got into college you've experienced smoother sailing. You seem to be hammering out a good life and have plans for your future. I know there will be more books after this one, along with other projects.

I honestly didn't think you would be able to go to college because of the state you were in during high school. But look at you now. You are only halfway through college and you already have a book coming out. How many people can say that?

In five years I have never seen somebody be as strong and grow up as fast and as much as you have. I love you for it.

Steven Karr
July 2013

INTRODUCTION

I HAVE WANTED TO WRITE A BOOK FOR A LONG TIME. The concept occurred to me during my road to recovery. Several of my therapists said that my life was at times complex, unbelievable, and a story that all should hear. I took that into consideration and looked through my journals. All of the fears, dreams and realities in them could be brought to life. This book is my best attempt of sharing what has happened so far in my twenty years.

I wrote this book for a few reasons. First, I wanted to help others. Many people around the world suffer from what

I have: depression, post-traumatic stress disorder, and anxiety disorders. I have had to fight these three every day of my life. I hope my experiences and suggestions can relieve people's pain.

Another motivation was to give clarity and light to speculation about my family and about myself. The histories of certain events needed to be cleared up. There are no hidden agendas in this book. In addition, I had no thoughts of revenge or of getting back at anyone. I wrote this book with nothing but good intentions. I did not write this book for attention, fame, or anyone's pity. I want no part of that.

Writing this almost killed me. Reliving everything that took place was incredibly painful and a torturous experience. At one point I thought about scrapping the entire project. The constant flow of ideas led to insomnia and some of the worst flashbacks I have ever had.

But a few people reminded me that if it was this painful to produce, I was doing something right.

This is the story of how I defeated my demons and my doubters.

IN NEED OF LOVE

CHAPTER 1
House of Horrors

August 2009

I WAKE UP WITH A HEADACHE AGAIN.

It's a warm day in August—the first day of my junior year at Bellarmine College Preparatory School. Junior year is pivotal when applying to colleges. Schools look to these semesters as a reflection of how one will do in college.

I open my eyes and they itch. I am still battling seasonal allergies and I hate it. My nose is constantly running, the crest of my mouth itches, and my eyes burn. I can hear my mom and my stepfather downstairs preparing breakfast. They always wake up very early and usually make a lot of noise.

I walk into the bathroom and turn on the shower. I undress, look at myself in the mirror, and step into the tub. This will be the highlight of my day, and I know it. The warm water rushes down my shoulders and past my legs. I let it consume me and I dream of escaping this prison I am trapped in. Every day I wake up with little energy and motivation to live. I rarely feel good anymore.

My goals for this school year are simple: get better grades than I did last year, become a little more outgoing, and try my best to make sure everything in my family is okay. If I can do all of that, I should survive. I need to do whatever I can to survive. Each day is a grind. There is pressure, stress, and we need to keep Mom happy. If Mom is not happy, our lives are horrible.

The house I currently live in is my house of horrors. The end of my life as I know it could take place here. I may die in this house. We will see if I make it through this year. I will be surprised if I do. I am already disintegrating.

I have drifted through the last five years. All of the scars are adding up. At this point my life is not worth living. It is mostly an exercise in frustration and pain. I never knew I could feel pain this deep. The hurt sears through my body and mind. Headaches, body aches and exhaustion own me. I submit to them and have lost the will to fight back.

CHAPTER 2
Start with What You're Given

I WAS BORN ON FEBRUARY 12, 1993, AT THE KAISER Permanente hospital in Santa Clara, California. Santa Clara is located about a half an hour south of San Francisco.

My parents were very young when they had me. My father was twenty-eight and my mother was a year younger. They met when they were teenagers and married when my father was twenty-three.

I have some fond memories from my childhood. Most of them revolve around athletics. Since I can remember,

I have always loved sports. I loved watching baseball, hockey and football with my Dad. We would sit on the couch every Sunday and watch football—usually the 49ers, our home team. It was so much fun. I had a difficult time falling asleep every Saturday night because I was so excited for the following day. Around nine the next morning *The NFL on Fox* pregame show would begin. I knew the theme song by heart.

My obsession with football continues to this day. In 1999 the 49ers beat the Green Bay Packers and advanced to the NFC divisional round against the Atlanta Falcons. That Sunday I was pumped up. I was six years old and this game meant a lot to me. When the 49ers ended up losing the game I was absolutely devastated. I ran into my room and shut the door. I sat down on my bed and cried my eyes out until I fell asleep. That is how much of a die-hard fan I was. I cannot believe my emotions were that strong when I was six.

I also remember going to my first 49ers game when I was eight years old. They played the St. Louis Rams, and Steve Young was quarterback. We had seats at the fifty-yard line and I could see everything. That afternoon was an amazing experience.

A year earlier I went to my first hockey game. That's when

I fell in love with the San Jose Sharks. Dad got seats right behind the penalty box from a company he worked with. He and my grandfather and I went to the game. I thrived on the energy in the building. The noise of the crowd was deafening and the pace of the players was fantastic to watch.

At the end of the game, something magical happened. A puck sailed over the glass and into the penalty box. The NHL employee who was working in the box turned around and looked directly at me. In his right hand was the puck. He tossed it to my grandpa, who handed it to me. I was so excited. I looked down at my right hand. *It's a used game puck! This has to be the best moment of my life so far.*

Ever since that day I have watch every single San Jose Sharks hockey game. I live and die each season with that team.

My family went to Disneyland all the time. I swear we were there every two months. Both sides of the family would come along. Each time we went it was a big event. I think that was the best part of the trips. Everybody who loved me was around me. I didn't have a worry in the world. I was happiest in "the happiest place on earth." I loved going there. All the magic and mystery of the park overwhelmed me. My favorite rides were Peter Pan and Pinocchio. I wanted to go on them a million times each day. If I was lucky, we would stay in the Disneyland Hotel. Those were the best nights of my childhood. Every morning we would hit up Goofy's Kitchen, a restaurant connected to the hotel, for breakfast. If I got the Mickey Mouse pancakes I was a happy camper.

I always loved Christmas. Nothing in the world made me more excited than waking up on December 25th. The family would come together, and we had a great time. My parents would always let us open one gift on Christmas Eve. I would always shake the box to see if I could get a better idea of what was in there.

One Christmas, our relatives from the United Kingdom visited and brought us gifts. I was expecting something fun that I could play with. I was only seven, so I was into Legos and stuff like that. When I opened the gift from them I began to cry. They had given me tighty-whitey underwear. I was so disappointed. *Why would they buy me these?* I thought. I already had enough underwear to last me a lifetime. I went upstairs crying.

To this day, I still don't know why I cried over the underwear. Maybe it was because my parents had set such high expectations during previous holidays. I pretty much got everything I wanted. It was ridiculous. I was so spoiled.

I would also cry after I'd opened all of my gifts on Christmas Day. I was so sad that the event was over. I loved the surprise of opening gifts. When all of that was over it was back to reality . . . which I never liked.

***

My father, John Fischler, was born on February 5, 1964, in upstate New York. He is the youngest child in his family. He has two older brothers, Peter and Mike. Peter is a wealthy bond trader who lives in Los Angeles. Mike is a producer in Hollywood who has also done well. My dad also has an older sister named Sue. She lives in England and has a Ph.D. in history from Oxford University.

So as you can see, the Fischler family is full of success. The expectations for me are high and I love it. I love the pressure that comes with being the oldest child. I have embraced it for a long time now and I thrive on it. I would not have it any other way.

There is no person I admire more in this world than my Dad. To most people he may seem typical. But believe me, there is nothing typical about my father. He knows me better than anyone else and is one of my best friends. What makes our relationship so great is the fact that he can act like a teenager as well as an adult. We laugh about things that are only funny to us. Most of the stuff we laugh about would probably offend most people. But that is the way we like it.

My Dad was a realtor for a very long time. He was quite successful at it, especially when the market was booming. He was raking in a good amount of dough and we were financially comfortable. But the economy spiraled downward after the events of September 11, 2001. The housing market was hit hard. This meant that my Dad needed to find another job.

Before he began his real estate career Dad had been a substitute teacher. He loved teaching physical education, and he enjoyed working with kids. He always has. That's why he coached my Little League teams, soccer teams, flag-football teams. . . . You get the point. The guy likes sports and teaching.

Dad eventually found a job at a Catholic K-through-8 school in west San Jose. He was making okay money, but most importantly he was enjoying himself. After a year at this school he was feeling pretty good. I could tell that he liked where he was and could see himself there for a long time.

Unfortunately, that never happened. In December of 2010 several girls in the sixth grade accused him of sexual harassment. There was an investigation that lasted for the entire month and it changed my Dad's life forever. As everyone already knew, there was no truth to these accusations. The school offered Dad his job back, but he respectfully declined. He didn't want to work in an environment where his reputation had been tarnished and every single one of his moves was being watched.

These accusations have absolutely destroyed my father. He is the not the same man he used to be. I can see it in his eyes. The trust he used to have in people has vanished. Since that December he has remain unemployed and has struggled to make ends meet. I don't know if he will ever fully recover from this event. Luckily he has a very supportive family and a wife who loves him.

What I hate most about what happened is that my father would slit his wrists before he would ever hurt a child. That's why these accusations hurt him so badly. He was doing something he loved and it was taken away from him. Trust me, I would know if my own father was a pedophile. He is the farthest thing from one.

Unfortunately, rumors started to swirl around San Jose. Several people told me that my Dad was a pedophile. I scoffed at these comments. They had no idea what was going on. My brother Max was also teased at school about Dad. I reach out to those who feel the need to make fun of my father. They must be very insecure about themselves if they attack an innocent man's children. Their behavior truly sickens me.

In the end my Dad may get the last laugh. In the near future there will be court dates that will decide how much money he will get for all the pain they put him through. Unfortunately, no amount of money will ever be able to make up for this tragedy. The Fischler family has been subjected to abuse, neglect, and tragedy. Those three words could be what define us. But I have a funny feeling that will not be the case.

My family is full of fight. We have this tendency to never go away. Like the fly you constantly swat at but can't kill. I like to think of that little guy as my family. There are so many times we all could have completely collapsed. The unit could have been in ruins and I would definitely be dead. But people such as my stepmother Brenda Lee, my therapists and others have breathed new life into us. Nothing seems to faze us anymore. All the quirks, horrific events and fights add to the lore of our family.

Every time my friends meet my family they are always surprised. We are different than everybody else. Sure, my Dad could be seen as more of a buddy than a father figure to me. But who cares? It works for us. We are doing pretty damn well at this point. I continue to prove the doubters and cynics wrong. The mentality this group has amazes me. The amount of fight left is astonishing for all the battles we have already gone through.

I think my stepmother Brenda is sometimes shocked at how much energy we have left. Even my best friend Steve has no idea how I do it. He gets frustrated and his family is pretty normal. Yes, we are weirder than most. Yes, we do things much differently than others. Do we care what the rest of the world thinks? Not so much. If we did, we wouldn't be the Fischlers. Fischlers never quit. We don't lie down when the world batters us blue. We continue to scratch and claw 'til the bitter end. You could put as at the bottom of a totem pole and I guarantee you we would find a way to the top. We might not have the best talent in the world. But as a five-person unit our competition level and work ethic can beat anyone's.

***

My mother was born to parents who were not highly educated. They came from poor families and both had difficult upbringings. But they made the best of the situation and worked as hard as they could to provide for their daughters. They opened up Caskey Country Club Properties in the eastern foothills of San Jose and had a lot of success.

My mother has two younger sisters. Rebecca, the middle child, is my favorite aunt. She loves me unconditionally and has been extremely supportive of every decision I have made in my life. The youngest sister, Gina, has lived an interesting life to say the least. She has been addicted to pills since college and has never really recovered.

Although I may speak ill of some of my family members, they have nevertheless provided some positive moments in my life. My grandparents are two of the most caring people in the world who want nothing but the best for me. They have taken me on some amazing trips to the British Virgin Islands and the Bahamas. They opened up my eyes to island life, which is not a bad lifestyle at all. Sitting on the beach, snorkeling during the day and dancing at night, is not a bad way to go through life. My aunt Rebecca is a caring woman who has been there for me since day one. She raised a great family of her own and understands what I have gone through.

Unfortunately, after I couldn't take the pain anymore and left my mother's house—which I'll tell you about in a bit—I was pretty disconnected from Mom's side of the family. My mother didn't want me to speak or even see them. The feeling was mutual. So for a good year I cut them out of my life.

***

I have two brothers. Their names are Zachary and Max. Zach is seventeen years old and is at St. Lawrence Academy in Santa Clara. Max is thirteen and attends Archbishop Mitty High School in San Jose.

My brothers had a different experience with my mother than I had. They don't remember most of the stuff that took place and they are better off for it. My relationships with them are quite complicated, though.

Zachary has always been different. I've known it since he was a toddler. He talked and acted differently than all my friends' siblings. I never knew why he was different. Thankfully our family gained some clarity on his condition: about a year ago he was diagnosed with Asperger Syndrome, a developmental disorder. Asperger's is tough to deal with. Zach takes every sentence I say literally, so I have to be careful.

According to his doctor he is a nine year-old in a seventeen-year-old body. To put this in perspective, I can have more adult conversations with Max then I can with Zach.

Zach also will never understand why I left home. He believes that family is the most important aspect of life. He is one of the most loyal people I know. Therefore, he often thinks that I have abandoned my mother. I have to remind him that this is not the case. I try not to badmouth his mom, but sometimes I have to in order to get my point across. There have been conversations where I get so frustrated with him that I leave the room. So our relationship has often been turbulent.

Max and I get along okay. He has always looked up to me and copied me. He copies what I say, what I do, and my attitude towards life. He tries his hardest to receive unconditional love and to make a connection with me. In the past I have found this incredibly difficult to handle. He crowds me and at times can be overbearing. I love the guy to death, but I need space. Recently I have begun to appreciate his admiration for me and tried to be a good influence on him. That said, my relationship with him has also been a struggle.

My brothers and I have had some good times, though. I will always love them unconditionally and until I die.

CHAPTER 3
The First Breakup

The earliest memory I have of my childhood is when my brother Max was an infant. I was an innocent seven-year-old who loved to have fun. That day, my Dad had gone to the gym to work out. Mom was left at home with us, and it may have been the scariest day of my life. Max kept crying and my mom could not get him to quiet down. She became so fed up with all of it that she locked us in our rooms and was going to leave. She kept crying and cursing Dad. I remember just sitting in my room. I was so scared and the tears started to come. Fortunately, Dad got home before Mom left, and he made us a nice dinner that night. Little did I know, my parents were well on their way to a divorce.

***

A few months later I watched my father chase my mother through the house. They were having some sort of fight and I saw the whole thing. Dad pinned Mom against the wall and they just kept screaming. Even though I was very young, I knew this was not a good sign.

They eventually divorced and told us about their decision while we were all on the back porch of our home. I could tell that Mom and Dad were both unhappy, and I remember the moment like it was yesterday. My brothers Zachary and Max really had no idea what was going on. They were only five and two at the time. My parents told us that we would be able to live in our home, but they would split time with us.

I had no idea that my life would be changed forever. My Dad moved into a condo about five minutes away, and my mom lived with one of her friends. Every year I had two birthday parties, two Christmases, and two Halloweens. Most kids thought this was a cool idea, but I really didn't like it. The custody situation was simple: my dad would be with us one week and mom would be with us the next. This didn't work out well at all. After that plan failed, Dad bought out Mom and gave her one of the homes that we owned on the block.

Mom had a tougher time adjusting to the divorce than Dad did. I remember her always being angry and sad. I think she was very lonely and didn't know what to do. The house she moved into was called a "rooming house." This meant that even though we owned the home, other people lived with us. There was an old man named Joel who lived upstairs, a woman named Laura who also lived upstairs, and a black woman whom I didn't know very well. I later found out that she was a prostitute. Very child-friendly, right?

For a long period of time my brothers and I slept in the same bed as my mom. We were all miserable and I hated being over there. Sharing a home with other people is not fun, especially when you are used to having your own room. I just wanted to go back to my dad's place and sleep in my own bed.

During this time I cried a lot. I had nobody to talk to about all this pain I felt from the divorce. I was one of the only kids in my class at school who had divorced parents.

Looking back on it, I don't think I understood the toll it took on me. I was only eight and I struggled with my emotions.

CHAPTER 4
Masks and Shadows

DURING THE NEXT FEW YEARS MY PARENTS BEGAN TO SEE other people. Dad dated a young, gorgeous girl named Leslie, and Mom dated a few different guys. I didn't like this at all. My parents seemed to be absorbed in their relationships and spent less time with us. Their attention was on their boyfriend or girlfriend instead of their kids. I know this may sound selfish, but my brothers and I weren't doing so well at the time. We needed a lot more support than we were getting.

One of the most bizarre moments in my life took place during Thanksgiving that year. My Dad brought Leslie to

Thanksgiving dinner up in Bolinas, a small town north of San Francisco. Both families had made a tradition of going up there since I was little. On Thanksgiving night I began thinking about Christmas. I always knew that Santa Claus was not real, but I wanted someone to confirm it for me. I asked Leslie if he existed. She told me he didn't and I was so happy. I immediately ran up to my mom and told her what I had just discovered. Boy, the information didn't sit well with her. She lost it.

"Well, obviously you want Leslie to be your mom, since you asked her about Santa first!"

The last intention I had was to hurt my mom's feelings. This was the first time I realized that mom was not normal. She reacted and absorbed situations much differently than everyone else. I would find out more about her "condition" as I grew older.

***

The next several years saw a pattern of abuse that took place in my mother's home. The abuse consisted of emotional blackmail, verbal jabs, and anything else she could do to make you feel guilty.

One night my brothers and I went to see a movie with Dad. In the past Mom had created a habit of "calling" movies so she could see them with us before Dad did. I think this was one of the first times I realized how low her self-esteem was at the time. She believed she had gotten dibs on the movie. When we came over and told her that we had already seen it with Dad, she got angry.

"How could you do such a thing to your own mother?" she said. "I'm disappointed in all of you. Especially you, Alex."

She could not believe that I would betray her like this. I was befuddled since I didn't think I'd done anything wrong. I just went and saw a movie with my Dad and thought nothing of it. She took it personally and used it as an opportunity to crush me.

My relationship with Mom was never the same after this. She started to question me often about how much I loved her. She would tell me that I didn't love her at all and I should go live at my dad's. These moments were brutal for me. We would all be sitting in the living room and she would give us a cold stare. She was convinced that none of her sons loved her. My two brothers really didn't know what to say to her. They were still too young to realize what was happening. I just told her that I did love her. I couldn't think of another response. What was I supposed to say in that moment to make her feel better?

These ordeals took place every week we were at her house. It really got out of hand. Her reasoning for these attacks was that a son who loved his mother would never disappoint her as much as I did. I tried to ignore these ridiculous claims as much as I could. But I was only nine years old so they started to sink in. Being questioned about your love for a parent hurts. Yes, I did love my Mom then. I told her a million times that I loved her. She never believed me. I tried as best as I could to meet her needs and be the best son I could be. None of my efforts were ever good enough.

I would often talk to my dad about what my mom said to me. I thought that none of my friends' mothers said these types of things to them. Being the great dad he is, he never said one bad word about my mom. He would just calm me down and put me at ease.

I dealt with similar verbal and emotional abuse for many more years. All of the criticism and guilt would eventually lead to deep depression.

CHAPTER 5
Two Relationships

WHEN I WAS ELEVEN I WAS INTRODUCED TO THE MAN WHO would eventually marry my mom. One day Mom told us we were going to drive to Santa Cruz to visit a friend of hers. After the forty-five minute, twisty-turny, ride down Highway 17, we found ourselves in front of a house. A man walked out and gave Mom a big hug. The hug looked to be more than one that "friends" would have. I quickly forgot about it and headed inside.

The man introduced himself and tried to act like he was my buddy. I was not buying his crap; too many other guys had tried to do the same thing. I walked into the living room and there was a blonde boy playing with some toys. This was the man's son. He was very shy and didn't seem interested in talking with us. To break the ice, the man suggested that we go outside and play some volleyball.

I must admit, we had a good time that day—a much better time than I thought we would have. It was getting dark and the man suggested that we make s'mores. I have always loved s'mores so I was beginning to warm up to this guy. His kid had started to open up and I realized we had a lot in common. He was the same age as Max and loved sports as much as we did.

The night was going well . . . until Mom said that we would spend the night there. I knew what that meant: she and the man were not "just friends." I slept in a room alone that night. I could hear voices coming from the living room. I decided to go see what they were doing. When I turned the corner I saw them kissing. I immediately ran back to my room and began to cry. I was homesick and wanted to talk to my dad. This was the beginning of one of the roughest periods of my life.

The man eventually moved in with us. This upset me to no end. At the beginning I thought he was cool. But once he moved in, he transformed into a cruel and heartless human being. He acted like he was our dad and that he actually knew what was best for us. He turned our house into a mini boot camp. Everything had to be done the way he wanted it to. If not, there would be hell to pay. He was always up my ass about something. I wanted to tell him to fuck off so many times.

His son also started to come over a lot more. I liked his son, though. We had a pretty good relationship. But I knew the inevitable was going to happen. This man was going to marry my mom. It was the last thing I wanted. None of my friends liked him, and neither did I.

A few months later Mom told me she was getting married. I told her I didn't approve, but she didn't seem to care. Later that week we went to lunch with my grandparents. The man stood up at the table and announced a couple of things. One, he and my mom were engaged. Two, he wanted to offer the position of best man in the wedding . . . to me. *Fuck*, I thought. *Really? He is going to play this card?*

Mom made me accept the offer, and it was set. The wedding would be on March 12, 2005. Coincidentally it was opening day for Little League baseball. I would miss playing in the first game of the season to watch some guy I didn't like marry my mom. Great.

To make things even worse, my dad had found another partner as well. She lived up in Danville, which is about forty-five minutes away from San Jose. The first time we met her she was a total sweetheart. She bought us treats and asked us a lot of questions. In addition, she was very pretty. She did a good job of acting like she cared about us. I totally bought into what she seemed to be.

Dad dated her for a year and then asked her to marry him. I thought this was a little rushed, and to this day he admits he felt pressured by my mother's remarriage. He was a little insecure after the divorce too.

So there I was, with both of my parents getting remarried. Here's the kicker, though: they were getting married within a month of each other. Dad was marrying this woman on April 17th. So in a span of two months my life would be drastically different.

CHAPTER 6
Two Weddings

My mom's wedding was a nightmare. For some reason she and the man decided to have the ceremony in my grandparents' basement. The room was packed and it was ridiculously hot in there. To make the day even odder, one of my friend's moms was the pastor. The ceremony ended quickly and I ran into the backyard. I needed to take a breath and regroup. I played some basketball with a couple of my friends who were there. Their presence really helped a lot. I don't think I could have made it through the day without them.

By the end of the day I was completely exhausted. I spent the night at my grandparent's house. My mom and her new man were off to some hotel in Santa Cruz. I went to sleep knowing things were not going to get better.

I didn't think my dad's wedding could be worse than my mom's. I didn't completely hate the person he was marrying . . . until that weekend.

The wedding was at the Ritz Carlton Hotel in Half Moon Bay, a town on the California coast, south of San Francisco. That was the best part of the wedding. If you have not been to Half Moon Bay, it is a beautiful place. The views of the coast from the hotel are spectacular.

My dad's wedding was much more put together than my mom's. It was this woman's first and she made it known that it would be perfect. From the ceremony to the food, everything would be the way she wanted it. I could see the stress radiating from her. It was scary. I had not seen that side of her before. Unfortunately I would see a lot more of it in the year to come.

The day was finally here. Our nanny Angelica helped my brothers and I put on our tuxedos. This was the second time we had done this in a month. It felt like we were just going through the motions. I went downstairs and took a seat near the door that led to where the guests were gathered. Several people came up to me and asked who I was. I was offended by these questions. *How can you not know that I'm one of the groom's sons? Do you not know that this woman's soon-to-be husband has kids?* What a joke.

The ceremony was fairly quick. Afterward my uncles took us up to the dining room. We waited forever as the bride and groom took a million pictures. (They would be divorced in a year. What a great waste of money.)

My dad and his new wife finally showed up. Here's what struck a nerve with me: Once we all sat down I realized that the table my brothers and I were at was not even close to my dad's. In fact, I couldn't see my Dad from my table. I was so disappointed. I felt left out and abandoned—almost as if my brothers and I were invisible that day.

I couldn't take any more. I ran into one of the recreation rooms on the first floor. I knew they had videogames in there so I could relax and not worry about anyone finding me. Of course, someone did.

The man that found me was Bud Geracie. Bud always seemed to find me. Bud had been my Little League coach since I was six, and he knew me better than anyone. I kept crying and he tried his best to settle me down.

"I hate this," I told him. "I want to leave."

Bud shook his head. "You can't, kid." He sat down next to me. "Why do you want to go?"

I couldn't really explain it to him. I was stressed out and worried about the future. My life seemed to be slipping away and there was nothing I could do about it.

Dad eventually came in and said that everything would be okay. I knew he could see how much pain I was in, and it hurt him too.

That night Angelica drove my brothers and me home. The worst was yet to come. . . .

CHAPTER 7
Two Marriages

EACH OF PARENTS' REMARRIAGES WAS QUITE DIFFERENT. One involved a woman who wanted to have a child. The other had two people who had already had children and were looking to have fun together. Unfortunately, both of these marriages turned out to be awful for everyone involved.

My Dad's marriage lasted one year, maybe a little less. The woman had decided that she didn't like living in downtown San Jose and wanted to move to a suburb. So my Dad bought a nice home in the Almaden hills. This purchase was by far the best part of their marriage. The house had a pool, a great view, a huge living room and many other amenities.

The only unfortunate part was that she was living there with us. She was one of the biggest control freaks I had ever met. This woman was a twin so she was always competing with her sister. How stupid is that? A few months after moving in, the woman's sister and husband came to visit. My brothers and I had to clean our rooms that morning before they arrived.

As I was cleaning my room, she came in. She noticed a small spot on my mirror. She asked if I would spray it and clean it up. I was fine with the request itself; my only problem was with her tone of voice. There was definitely a snap to it and I didn't like that at all. So I decided not to clean my mirror. Thirty minutes later she came back into my room to check on my work. Being the tight-ass she was, she noticed the fucking spot. She then proceeded to yell at me, which I disliked even more. I ended up washing the mirror and she thanked me profusely.

The biggest problem I had with this woman was how fake she was. Fake tits, fake smile, fake first impression, fake *everything*. She was the definition of a fraud. Living with her hurt all of us. The house was a very stressful place. The results of all this stress could be seen in my Dad. He gained a ton of weight and looked exhausted.

The best moment of their entire marriage came the following August. The woman and Dad told us to come downstairs. She started to cry. That is when I made a fist pump. I knew what was happening. I had gone through it before. They were getting a divorce and I couldn't be any happier. She was finally out of our lives. The nightmare had lasted only a year.

After this great announcement we went to the grocery store. My brothers and I kept telling my Dad how relieved we were that he had ended it with her. He shared the same feelings. He looked like the weight of the world had been taken off his shoulders.

***

As I said, I was never a fan of my mother's new husband. He probably never should have been a father. He was mistreated by his own parents, so he had no idea how to treat children. Two years into their marriage, his son didn't return to our house one week. My brothers and I asked what had happened to our stepbrother. Mom tried to make us believe that the man's ex-wife had turned his son against him.

The truth? That wasn't the case at all. The son was taken away because his father had abused him in multiple ways. I saw some of this abuse in person. One time the man pulled his son, who was misbehaving, by the collar and shoved him against a wall. In addition, the man was always very harsh with his son and demeaned him often.

Looking back on it the relationship between my mother and her new husband was awful. No wonder his son wanted to leave.

All of this led to a family therapist visiting our house one day. Mom told us just to act normal. I figured it was no big deal, and the therapist only stayed for about an hour. Mom said that the man was there to see how great our family was, so that our stepbrother could come back. (Since I haven't seen my stepbrother since 2008, I am guessing the therapist didn't think it was that great. I will probably never see my stepbrother again.)

Once his son left, the man redirected some of the abuse toward my brothers and me. A year before I left the house for good I saw him hit Max. We had just returned from a lake trip the week before, and it was time to wash the boat.

Max was not putting in the effort that our stepdad wanted. So he slapped Max across the back of the head. Max began to cry. I told him to come over and I just hugged him. I must admit that I was scared during that moment. This guy's kid had already been taken away from him. Who knew what he was capable of doing?

The drive back to San Jose was a little nerve-wracking to say the least. Once we got back home I told my Mom about what had taken place. I was expecting her to react angrily toward her husband. But there was really not that big of a reaction at all. She told him to not do it again and asked Max if he was okay. That was it. Her son had just been slapped across the back of the head, and she acted like everything was fine. This blew me away.

Another example of this abuse occurred when the man was coaching Max's Little League team. Max was playing second base and made a few fielding errors during a game. The man screamed at Max multiple times that day. It got so bad at one point that the umpire came up and warned him that if he spoke to Max like that one more time, he would not be coaching anymore.

Besides being very cruel to Max, the man was also mistreated me. Most of my friends knew that from an early age I had wanted to be a sports journalist. I announced at a family dinner during my junior year of high school that I would be pursuing a journalism degree. I said that I wanted to cover hockey or another major sport. The man decided to make a joke at my expense. "Alex," he said, "the only thing you'll ever cover professionally is the rodeo."

Everyone at the table started to laugh. I didn't find it funny at all. I promised myself that I would prove all of them wrong.

The man overstepped his boundaries again on Halloween of my junior year in high school. I was taking some difficult classes that semester. I had decided to stay home and do homework instead of going out with my friends that night. My mom and stepfather asked if I was going out to any parties. I told them no—there were not many parties since it was a weekday. Once again, he decided to crack a joke:

"Oh, there are parties Alex, you just don't know where they are," he said.

I didn't know what he was trying to imply—maybe that I was a loser or was not popular. He and my mom always made fun of me in front of my friends. They seemed to really enjoy it. I just thought, *This must be some more of their crap*. I ignored him.

These rifts between him and me would continue until I left for college. My relationship with this guy was really off and on. At times he could be really cool. He even took me to a Giants game, where I got to go on the field and watch batting practice. I could also talk sports with him as well. But living with him was a different story. As I mentioned earlier, he wanted everything to be perfect. Every chore had to be done to his standards. I think what bugged me the most was the fact that he acted like he was our dad. He disciplined us like he was our dad, talked to us like he was our dad, and often tried too hard. I got sick of his act very quickly and he was a big reason why I left home.

***

Mornings were always the worst time of the day while I was living at Mom's. She and her husband were always loud in the morning, and it was unbearable. I would wake up with itchy eyes and a stuffy nose. My allergies were always worse there than at Dad's, and I never understood why. Anyway, her husband would bang on the door to wake me up in the morning.

"Hey Alex, wake up!"

It was the most annoying thing in the world. I resented him so much. I wanted to respond with obscenities but chose not to.

After this disturbing wake-up call I would shower. Under the water I would think about how miserable I was. I would often cry in the shower because I knew nobody would be able to notice the tears when I came down the stairs.

This happened every morning. I hated my life and what it had become. I was living under a roof where nobody loved me. I wanted to kill myself. I thought about it every day during my junior year. I contemplated just ending it. I had nothing to live for. High school was a bore and my mother and her husband constantly squashed my hopes for the future. I despised going back to their house every other week.

The life I had at my Dad's was the life that I wanted. He gave me the independence I longed for, and he believed in me. I deserved both of those from Mom and her husband. I was a great kid up to that point. I had never drunk alcohol, touched a drug or gotten into trouble. Most of my friends can attest to that. I was scared of those substances and what they could do to me. There was a moment during my sixteenth birthday at a hotel I will always remember. We met some guy in the elevator and my buddies told him it was my birthday. He said he had some girls back at his place we could talk to. Being the dumb kids we were, we followed this guy up to his room. In the bathroom sink were sixty bottles of Corona beer sitting on ice. In addition, there were two prostitutes relaxing in the room and a ton of weed stacked on the nightstand.

I started to panic. I didn't feel comfortable being in this guy's room. Some of my other friends felt fine. They smoked weed with him and talked to his girls. One of my friends even demanded that I stay there with them. I looked him right in the face and said no. He was shocked that I had put my foot down like that. I was usually the one in the group who was pretty easygoing and up for anything. But during that point in my life I was against drugs and alcohol. Ironically they would both become things I would depend on in the future.

A few moments later I took the elevator back down to the lobby. Mom and one of her co-workers were talking. I told Mom what had happened. I will never forget her response.

"It is okay, Alex. You have to try new things."

I was stunned. Mom was basically saying she wanted me to try these substances. I had no idea why she would say that. That is not the usual response that a kid receives from his parent. Most of my friends' parents would not be okay with them smoking weed and drinking at sixteen years of age. I guess my Mom was different.

CHAPTER 8
Balls

BETWEEN MY FRESHMAN AND SOPHOMORE YEAR OF HIGH school, Dad introduced me to the sport of racquetball. He thought it would be a great way to relieve some of the stress I was dealing with. Racquetball also burns a ton of calories, and I needed to lose some weight.

I started playing with some of the old guys (the regulars—these guys have been playing there for years!) at the San Jose Athletic Club. At first, nobody wanted to play with me since I was really bad. I had a tough time returning serves and positioning myself correctly. I started taking some lessons from a few different pros and started to improve. I was also playing every day after school, so that helped. Eventually I beat some of the guys at the club. My shot management and game management were much better. I had also gained some racquet speed and gotten a little quicker. All of these ingredients led to a lot of success on the court.

My Dad and I played in our first tournament in Bakersfield, California. I played Cs singles and Cs doubles with him. For those who do not know how the ranks of racquetball work, it's pretty simple: Pro, Elite, A, B, C, and D. So at that time I was still a pretty bad player. I lost my first singles match and was pretty upset with myself.

My Dad ended up winning the C singles division. He has bragged about that win to this day. In doubles we did pretty well too. We won a match and I was satisfied. I also met a girl I would eventually take on a date. What I didn't know was that she was one of the top ten women racquetball players in the world. I knew she was good, but *wow*.

***

After my first tournament I knew I had to get better at the game. I took some lessons with Gene Pare. Gene is a world champion and has won many different titles. He is a class act and a real ambassador of the sport.

I owe so much to Gene. I consider him to be a surrogate father to me. He has taught me a great deal about racquetball, life and how to be a good person. I try my best to follow his teachings in every facet of my life. He taught me to be a gracious winner, a student of the game, and more importantly a great friend. He is the type of person who helps others and expects nothing in return.

All the hard work I put in finally started to pay off. Dad and I won the C doubles division at a tournament up in Concord, near San Francisco. Eventually I won a few state titles in my divisions and am now an All-American as a student at the University of Missouri.

I want to thank Louie, Evatt, Danny, Don, Dennis, Sergio, Eddy, Pat, Steve Simler, and anybody else I played against at the San Jose Athletic Club. These guys were patient with me as I grew into the player I am today. They also gave me a great deal of advice. I will always cherish those days at the club. I loved going there for two hours every day and having a blast.

Racquetball has done so much for me. It's one of the only stress releases I have. I am able to go out and put one hundred percent of my body and soul into winning a game.

Most people will tell you I am pretty intense on the court and tend to go all out, all the time. That's just the way I need to play to be successful. When it comes to any of my work in general I put everything I have into it. It's no different with racquetball.

CHAPTER 9
Spinning

As I grew older, my Mom's behavior became weirder.

In eighth grade I had a parent-teacher conference at the beginning of the year. Mom was running late, so my dad and I talked to my teacher first. She said that I was a great student but she would appreciate if I talked a little less in class. She added that the class as a whole talked too much and that she was going to bring it up the next day with all of us. I came away from the conference feeling pretty good about myself.

Mom came in about ten minutes later, and Dad and I waited for her to finish up with the teacher. When she was done, Mom came out and was very upset.

"Your teacher told me that you're a huge problem in class and that you're a disruption," she said.

The teacher had said nothing like that to us. Dad went back in and talked to the teacher. She told Dad that she had said the same thing to Mom that she had said to us. She did not understand how that was the conclusion Mom came to after their discussion.

This was the first instance since Thanksgiving dinner— where she freaked out when my dad's girlfriend revealed that Santa Claus wasn't real—that I realized there was something wrong with my mom. She took the information she was given and spun it however she wanted to. I didn't understand why she would do this.

Before I got to Bellarmine College Preparatory school, my parents had a dispute about tuition. Mom let it be known that Dad was the problem and that because of him I would not be attending Bellarmine. I was upset at my Dad and wanted to confront him about it. Fortunately I didn't have to. He knew me well enough to know that something was wrong with me.

We were in Arizona, celebrating my thirteenth birthday. The San Francisco Giants play pre-season baseball games in Scottsdale in March of every year, and my dad brought me down to watch spring training. One night after returning from a game we sat in our hotel room and watched a movie. Dad asked me if I wanted to talk. I did, and I told him what my mom had said.

"That is not what is happening here, Alex," he replied. "You are going to Bellarmine and you have nothing to worry about."

I felt relieved. A few months later I was off to Bellarmine to start high school. Once I got to there, Mom became even more controlling.

CHAPTER 10
Demons

DURING SOPHOMORE YEAR OF HIGH SCHOOL, EVERYTHING changed. I started to talk to a lot of girls and spend more time with my friends than I did with my family. Once I started dating a girl named Amanda, Mom became very paranoid. One day I was hanging out with Amanda and we decided to go over to her house to have brunch with her family. I decided not to tell my Mom since I was fifteen and it was a Sunday. Besides, I had nothing else to do.

Mom kept calling me on my cell and I eventually picked up the phone. She demanded to know where I was. I told her I was at Amanda's house having brunch. She lost it. She started screaming and told me she would drive down and pick me up immediately.

Amanda walked back with me to downtown Willow Glen, a neighborhood in San Jose. We kissed for the first time . . . and then my Mom came by and picked me up. She gave me the silent treatment in the car. I knew I was in trouble. The rest of the day there was a lot of tension in the house. Mom didn't speak to me the rest of the day. I knew this was not good.

The next morning I woke up and headed downstairs for breakfast. When I sat down there was a contract, typed on a piece of paper, lying on my plate. It was from Mom. The contract was about a paragraph long and said that she was disowning me. There were two horizontal lines at the bottom of the sheet of paper. This was where we could both sign to make it official. In the contract Mom stated reasons that were completely ridiculous and made no sense at all. Most of the reasons had to do with her insecurities. She said that I didn't love her and that she wanted nothing to do with me. This was because I would not share any of the details of my life with her.

I thought, *Wow, this is silly. I am a teenage boy; most teenage boys do not talk with their parents very much.* As I read the contract I laughed. This was insane!

Mom walked by the table and said, "Are you going to sign it?"

"No." I replied.

She glared at me. I had nothing to say to her. This was the moment that changed the relationship I had with my mother forever. I would not forgive her for this. I didn't deserve that contract at all. No child should ever get a contract from his parents saying they want to disown him. I had not done anything wrong. She needed to realize that I was becoming my own person. I decided to visit my therapist at school and tell him what had happened. When I walked into his office I immediately broke down. All of the stress had started to tear at me. I told him what had happened and he could not believe it. He had not heard a story this stupid before. He didn't understand why Mom had written a contract.

Since it was December and final exams were coming up, my therapist and I decided that the best thing for me to do was stay at my Dad's house. He helped me write an email to my mom, saying that once she cooled down I would return to her house and talk it through.

This set off a bomb.

My Dad was waiting to pick me up when school ended. Mom, however, had decided to send my grandpa over to Bellarmine to pick me up. Grandpa said that I was going with him and I didn't have a choice. The problem was I didn't have the authority just to leave my Mom's house and stay with my Dad. According to the custody regulations set up by the court, I had to be with her that week. So I ended up going to my grandparents' house. The car ride with my grandpa back to their house was very awkward. He knew that I was angry, and he tried to justify my mother's actions.

This is what everyone has tried to do since the day I left her house: justify everything that she did for me. They told me that she did all of those bad things because she loved me. It's all bullshit. You cannot terrorize your children because you love them. That's not the way it works. If you love your child you do what is best for him or her. My Mom always did what was best for her. She is one of the most selfish human beings I know. All of her decisions are based on what she wants, and she doesn't seem to care how her actions affect others.

Mom arrived at my grandparents' place after she got off work. I was in the basement crying and hiding because I didn't want to see or talk to her. She came downstairs and asked me what was wrong. She said that I had made her write that letter with all the mean things I had done to her.

Let's see, what's wrong here? First, I was a fourteen-year-old kid and she was in her forties. She should have been able to keep her emotions in check. There will never be a justification for why she wrote that letter. I don't care if she had a bad day or was frustrated with her life. You never, ever, say anything like that to your child. A mother is supposed to provide her child with unconditional love and support. My Mom's love has always come with conditions. If you do what she wants or says, then she will love you. She has a "you're either on my side or you're not" type of mentality. If you are not on her side, she will hold a grudge like no other.

This type of mindset is unhealthy and wastes a lot of energy. She never apologized for writing that letter. She never accepted responsibility for her actions. That's why I will never be able to have a relationship with her. She will never understand how badly those words hurt me. If I had deserved them, then so be it. But I didn't, and never will, deserve them.

***

Life at my mom's house only became worse after the contract. She and my stepdad were not letting me work out because it interfered with dinner. I usually went to the gym from 4 to 6 p.m. to play racquetball. They announced that dinner would be at five every night and I had to be there no matter what. I thought this was dumb. I was a high school kid who should be involved in activities after school. Who demands that their child be home at 5 p.m. for dinner? I was very frustrated with both of them. They didn't understand where I was coming from.

So one day after school the two of them came in to talk to my therapist. I started the meeting by saying that my needs at home were not being met. I also said that during the last two weeks at their house I had not been allowed to work out. I will never forget my Mom's response.

"I let him work out whenever he wants," she spat. "I have no idea what he is talking about."

I was stunned. She had blatantly lied to my therapist. I was so angry that I just opened the door and left. My dad was waiting outside since I was at his house that week. He asked me what was wrong and I told him what she had done. He shook his head in disbelief and that was it. I knew if I wanted to live my life I would have to leave my mom's house. I just needed to muster up enough courage to do so.

I never thought that my situation at her house could get much worse. But once I got my driver's license the tension escalated quickly. The first week I had my license I started driving to school. I drove the giant blue Chevy Suburban that had been in the family since I was very young.

One day I stayed after school in the library to finish some homework. Around 3:45 p.m. I headed over to the gym to play some racquetball. After I played a few games I checked my cell phone. I had six missed calls from Mom. Why had she called me six times? I called her back and she didn't pick up. I went outside to get better reception and noticed that the Suburban was missing from its parking space. I started to panic because I thought the giant SUV had been stolen.

I looked down and my phone was vibrating. Mom was calling.

"Um, why did you call me six times?" I asked her.

"I didn't know where you were, Alex," she said. "You scared me."

"Mom, my car is gone."

"I know it is. I took it."

"Why would you take my car?"

"Because I wanted you to feel the same way I did when I was panicking," she said. "I had no idea where you were."

"You obviously knew where I was," I said. "You took my car!"

She told me to walk home. I told her I would get a ride from one of the racquetball guys, and I hung up. This may have been the angriest I have ever been in my life. *Why would she take my car?* I didn't do anything wrong. I felt like she must not trust me at all.

I went back into the gym and played some more racquetball. I eventually got a ride home and nervously anticipated what I would face when I got there. Both of my ex-parents were waiting at the dinner table. They looked at me like I had just killed someone.

"You disobeyed us and you got what you deserved," said Mom.

"I have no idea how you think that," I said. "You don't trust me."

"No, we trust you. You just disobeyed us. You need to learn."

"I disagree with you," I said and walked away.

I sat in my room for the rest of the night. The anger started to build. I was being treated unfairly and it was getting out of hand. There was no reason for them to take my car away. I went to the gym like I did every day. They knew where I was; they were not scared.

***

Another incident I will always remember also occurred during junior year in high school. In my English class we were assigned a research paper. Our teacher suggested that we go to the library to find some sources. I thought that I should go to the Martin Luther King library near my house. It is one of the biggest libraries in the area and it would definitely have what I needed to start the paper. Before I went, I stopped at home to get a quick bite to eat. I couldn't find a parking space on our block, so I pulled into our driveway. I went into our house and my stepdad was there. He asked why I had parked in the driveway, and I explained my reason.

"Find a space on the street," he said. "Your mom is coming home and has to park in the driveway."

I reluctantly agreed and hopped back into my car. I drove around the block again . . . and still nothing had opened up.

Fuck it, I thought. *I might as well just go to the library.*

A few hours later I finished my work and returned home. But as I was thinking about the rest of the homework I needed to get done, I remembered something: I'd left my U.S. history book at my dad's house earlier in the week. I figured I would stop by and grab it before dinner. I parked in front of my dad's house and went up to my room. I used the bathroom and looked for my book. I'd forgotten where I had put it.

My phone began to vibrate. Mom was calling me.

"Why are you at your dad's, Alex?" she said. "I thought you said you were going to be at the library."

"I was. I just had to stop by to grab a book."

"I think you are lying to me again, Alex."

"Mom, I swear I am not."

"I think you are trying to abandon me," she said. "You just want to go live with your dad. Is that what you are doing over there? Hatching a plan to leave me?"

"No, Mom. That is definitely not the case."

"I don't believe you, Alex. Hopefully you'll come home."

She hung up. I looked at the phone and laughed. *What was that?* I thought to myself. *How could she think I was hatching a plan with Dad when he wasn't even home?*

She was becoming more and more paranoid. Each week

it seemed to get worse. I returned home that night and was given the silent treatment. This was usually followed with verbal abuse and a severe lowering of my self-esteem.

"You act this way because you do not love me."

"I wish you were more like your friends, Alex." (Meaning that they were better sons than I was.)

The next morning she still wouldn't talk to me. I began to feel even worse about my relationship with her. I knew that all of this drama was starting to kill me. My grades were starting to slip and I was not enjoying my life anymore. I needed to make a change . . . and soon.

CHAPTER 11
Love, or What I Thought It Was

I REMEMBER WHEN I STARTED DATING IN HIGH SCHOOL. I'd always been a shy guy and was rarely willing to approach a girl in public. Luckily there was a website called MySpace.com, which made my social life a lot easier. I was able to connect with friends and girls online. It was much easier than going about making friends and asking out girls in person.

During my sophomore year I went to many San Jose Sharks hockey games. I spent most of the game looking for girls my age. I'd often make eye contact with a few of these girls but I never had the balls to talk to any of them.

During one game a brunette in the lower bowl caught my eye. I was sitting with my friend Tommy Glasscott in section 104. For those who have never been to the HP Pavilion in San Jose (now called The SAP Center at San Jose), that's in the corner on the end where the Sharks attack twice— shooting at the opposing team's net twice. Teams switch ends after each period.

This girl I was staring at was sitting in section 102 in the same row. She was about twenty feet away from us. I caught her glancing at me a few times. She looked a bit familiar.

"Hey," I said to Tommy, "who is that girl in section 102 in our row?"

"Which one?" he said.

"The one in the white throwback jersey with a sweatshirt underneath."

"That's Amands Nichols," Tommy said. "She is a junior at Presentation."

Presentation was the all-girl high school in Willow Glen. I had been there only once, for the first dance of my high school career, and probably the least memorable dance I ever attended. I remember that night being very awkward as everyone stood around and talked to one another as music blasted in the background.

I asked Tommy if he had her cell number. He gave me a "what the hell?" look and I figured that was a no.

At the time, MySpace was a very popular Web site and an easy way to contact cute girls. The night after the game I logged on and looked up Amanda. I was in luck: she had an account and I could message her. I sat at my computer for a few moments debating what to say. This was one of the first times I'd attempted to talk to a girl that didn't attend St. Martin of Tours, my grade school. So, like a creeper, I sent the following message:

Hey! Were you sitting in Section 102 at the Sharks game tonight?

Right as I pressed send I felt like a moron. Who says that kind of thing to someone they have never met?

Anyway, I went to school the next morning anticipating a response by the end of the day. Of course I didn't receive one and I felt a sense of disappointment and failure. This is the way I felt most of my time in high school. That night I went to bed while listening to depressing love songs on my iPod.

The next day I woke up and immediately checked my phone. I had a MySpace message! My heart started to race as I waited for the slow-paced Internet on my phone to load the message. I can't remember exactly what Amanda said, but it was along the lines of, *Yes, that was me with the jersey/ sweatshirt combo in section 102.* I was excited when I read that response. I took a few minutes to digest the words. On the way to school I wrote her back.

We continued sending each other MySpace messages for a few days, and somehow I ended up with Amanda's phone number. We had some great texting conversations and she seemed to like me.

A week later I asked her out, and so it began: my first attempt at a high school relationship. I told her to meet me at Pizza My Heart in downtown San Jose around 7 p.m. Every Friday at Bellarmine College Prep the school day ended at 12:45. *Thank God.* The anticipation and nerves I had that day were ridiculous. This was my first date of my life and it was with an older girl! I must admit I felt a bit proud of myself. You don't see a sophomore boy taking out a junior girl every day.

As 6 p.m. rolled around I started to get dressed. I don't remember what I wore. I just recall looking in the mirror and having a sense of confidence I had never felt before.

Since as early as I can remember I have always liked to arrive early to any event or date. That night my mom dropped me off around 6:30. So that meant I had about a half-hour to play with my phone while looking for other cute girls. I sat in the end booth in the restaurant and began to screw around on my Razr phone. I was nervous as hell and the time was passing too slowly.

By 7 p.m. Amanda was still not there and I'd started to freak out. My hands were sweaty and I thought that she had stood me up. Just as I dialed my home phone number to ask Mom to pick me up, I got a text. It was from Amanda.

Be there in ten. Sorry!

I felt relieved and sat back down in the booth. I took a napkin and wiped the sweat off my hands. Amanda arrived about fifteen minutes later with an apologetic look on her face.

"I am so sorry!" she said. "I feel so bad."

"It's okay," I said. "Not the first time."

Well, that was a lie. It *was* the first time. But why should I tell her I'd never been on a date before, right?

After we ordered I began to feel tense. My hands began to sweat again and my words started to come out jumbled. I was nervous and had no idea what to do. *I cannot screw this up*, I thought. I had worked so hard to get this date. I let her know I had to go to the bathroom and I would be right back.

In the men's room I turned on the faucet and let the water run. I looked in the mirror.

"Get yourself together!" I yelled.

I washed the sweat off my hands and took a deep breath. I walked out and felt like I had some control. *Just ask her questions and don't talk about yourself,* I thought. So that's exactly what I did.

I had a few good times with Amanda. The relationship didn't last very long because I was an emotional wreck. I was very dependent on her and needed her attention all the time. I needed someone to confide in and trust, especially a girl. She got sick of this and ended up breaking up with me. I honestly deserved it. I had a rough couple of months during this time, especially with my mom. But I want to thank Amanda for everything. We had many good laughs and some fun during the time we spent together.

***

I first met Claire Thomas at St. Martin of Sunnyvale. My mom taught sixth grade, and Claire was in the class. She was pretty shy and we didn't really talk to each other much. Once we got to high school our paths crossed again. I asked her out and we started to date. I talked to her almost every day and things were going well.

I remember thinking that the relationship could actually go somewhere. But a few days later Claire told me she was very sick and needed to focus on herself. I thought she was full of shit and was just trying to find an easy way to end things. I moved on, but I carried a lot of anger toward her. I didn't understand why she didn't just say she didn't reciprocate my feelings. It made no sense.

A year later we started to talk again. My feelings of anger and hurt had simmered down, and I figured, what the hell? We went out again and she revealed why she had to end things one year prior. She *was* really sick and spent some time in the hospital.

I felt like a total asshole. I apologized for the way the things I had said to her and the way I acted. Surprisingly enough, she forgave me and wanted to start dating again. She even came to one of my racquetball tournaments that year.

One of the funniest moments in our relationship occurred in Livermore at her mom's apartment. Claire had been waiting a while for me to kiss her. Earlier that night she had asked me to her junior prom. I was so honored that she had asked me. No girl had done anything that special for me. I felt wanted and appreciated for one of the first times in my life. I knew she really wanted me to, but I was really nervous.

As I walked to the door to head home, she said, "Well, are you gonna kiss me?"

I laughed and then slowly moved in.

I thought it was a pretty good kiss and I walked to my car with a huge smile on my face.

Our relationship was moving along just fine until her prom night. I could tell she had some anxiety and it was making me uncomfortable. She did look beautiful in her navy blue dress though. After we took what seemed like a million pictures, we took a limo into downtown. The best part of this prom was that it was taking place at a familiar place: the second story of the gym where I played racquetball. The upper floors held events throughout the year and the prom was one of them. I relaxed a bit more since I was in familiar surroundings. I also had a few friends who were there as well.

As the night went on, I began to feel nervous. One of her friends pulled me aside and let me know that Claire was pissed off at me.

"No shit," I said.

"She wants you to kiss her, Alex!"

I knew it. I was not being the date that she had wanted me to be. I needed to step up.

I took her onto the dance floor and finally kissed her. A smile instantly came to her face and everything seemed to be looking up.

After the dance we stayed the night at a friend's house. Claire and I made out most of the night and slept on the couch together. We had a lot of fun and I will always remember that night.

The next morning, everything started to unravel.

My Dad called and said he was out front waiting for me. I had given him the address the night before so he could pick me up. I started to give Claire a kiss goodbye and she turned her head so all I could kiss was her cheek. On the ride home with my dad, I received a text from her.

Don't tell anybody what we did last night.

I was confused. Why would she not want anyone to know about us?

During the next week and a half she distanced herself from me. It was obvious that she didn't want to talk to me. I called her a few days later and told her that I wanted to break up. She was not going to commit to me, so I thought there was no point in going forward with this.

That phone call lasted three hours. I remember that detail because I missed the entire Sharks hockey game that night. The call ended with her crying as I said goodbye to her.

A week went without us talking. I then got a call from her after school. She left a message saying she wanted to talk. I called her back a few hours later and I said I would meet her at school that Friday. That may have been the biggest mistake I ever made. She didn't want to get back together with me. She just wanted to make it look like I didn't dump her. I was upset with her that entire weekend. In fact, I didn't talk to her for the rest of high school.

During that relationship I went through a lot of issues. The stress of dating Claire took its toll. I lost twenty pounds and was throwing up often. I learned later that this was due to my anxiety. My body was telling me that I had to end this. These signs would play a major role with the next girl I dated.

***

During the summer of my junior year I made a few mistakes—mistakes that were one hundred percent my fault and could have been easily avoided.

One of my major mistakes occurred with a girl I had liked for many years. I had fought over her in the past with one of my friends. She was a cute latina with dark brown hair, brown eyes and a gorgeous body. Her personality was easy to get along with.

It was July in San Jose, a hot one. I was spending a lot of time with my friend Tommy, and that meant one thing: girls, girls, girls. They would come over all the time and spend the night.

I was in a pretty deep depression then, and I tried to use girls as a coping mechanism. Tommy went to work early one day and I was stuck alone with two girls at his house. One of them suggested that we take a nap in his bed.

Okay, let's pause here for a second.

If two girls ask you to take a "nap" in the same bed, you always say yes, especially if they are cute like these were. This was the opportunity of a lifetime. We all lay down in the bed and started to cuddle. They both put their hands on my chest. God, I was in heaven. This was unbelievable. The girl I had always had a crush on was sleeping to my left. My leg was in between her two legs. I won't go into details, but some fooling around did take place. All of this happened while the other girl was sleeping. Once she woke up she asked why I was breathing so hard. My answer was a classic that I will never forget:

"Dust allergies. They affect my lungs."

I lied right through my teeth. I had no other choice.

The girls left thirty minutes later since one of them had to get home. A few moments later the girl who had slept through everything sent me a text:

Allergies, my ass!

I guess the brunette had told her what really happened. Of course, being a guy, I told my friends what took place. They were surprised but gave me the usual guy support. I was pretty happy with myself.

A few days later the brunette sent me a text. She said her boyfriend was out of town and she wanted me to drive to Gilroy, the "Garlic Capital of the World," to hang out with her. I was nervous and didn't know what to think of this situation. I was not the type of guy who liked to sneak around. But I was stupid so I drove to Gilroy. Luckily her little brother was home so I had to behave myself. The brunette and I walked to a park and talked while her little brother enjoyed himself on the playground.

While we were at the park the brunette's boyfriend called her and asked her if she was with anyone. She covered up the mic on the phone.

"Should I tell him you are with me?" she asked.

"Do whatever you want," I said. It's your boyfriend."

She gave me an odd look.

"I'm alone with my brother," she said into the phone.

She had lied to her boyfriend and this made me uncomfortable. We spent forty-five minutes at the park, and I told her I had to leave.

On the drive back to San Jose I thought about her. I didn't feel good about seeing or talking to her. I decided I would end all communication. This was not a safe situation to be in. Plus her boyfriend went to my school, so I would see him in a month when the school year started. I couldn't look that guy in the face without telling him what I had done. (That moment did come about in August, but I was able to keep it to myself. But I still felt horrible about what I had done.)

I ran into the brunette two months later and she ignored me. I didn't understand what her deal was. One of my friends told me that she believed that I'd spread rumors about her. This was completely untrue. I had just shared with my buddies what had taken place that day in bed. I guess she didn't want that information leaked to anyone since she had a boyfriend.

Well, you win some and you lose some. This was one girl I would never be able to talk to again. To this day I still have not talked to her, and she still hates me. I don't I can do anything to change her mind. I want to let her know I am sorry and am always willing to talk. I care about her and will always consider her a friend, even if she does not reciprocate.

***

I took a break and stopped talking to girls for a few months. I needed some time for self-reflection. I was a mess and was ready for the summer to start. I continued to play racquetball every day and hung out with my friends.

One night in late July I threw a party at my mom's house. I would never have guessed that it would be one of my last nights there. A good bunch of my friends came over and in walked a beautiful blonde. She had an amazing smile and an even better body. I was stunned. One of my friends told me that she was his and that I should stay away from her. But that only made me want her more. The next day I added her on Facebook. I told her to text me when she had time.

I got a text from her the next day. I asked her if she was really into my friend and she told me no. I know this goes strongly against guy code, but I asked her out. My friend was going on a two-week trip and I figured that taking her out was harmless.

We met downtown at the Fairmont hotel and had lunch at Johnny Rockets. The conversation was good so I decided we would head back over to the Fairmont. We sat in the foyer and talked for another hour. I was making her laugh, which I knew was a good thing.

I really enjoyed that date with her. It may have been one of the best dates of my life. There were rarely any awkward moments and she was so easy to talk to. I asked her out again and this continued. We had a lot of fun over those two weeks. I realized that I would eventually have to tell my friend what was happening. When he got home from his trip, I called him. I let him know what had taken place and he freaked out. I thought this could have ended our friendship. But after we talked for a long time he understood. He supported me and was happy if I was happy.

A few weeks later I asked the blonde to be my girlfriend. I remember that moment vividly. I was walking her out from my best friend's birthday party. I kissed her and said that I had a question to ask her. I think she pretty much knew it was coming. She said yes and I was back in another relationship.

When I look back on it, this was probably not the brightest move I have ever made. I was an emotional wreck and was hooked on prescription pills. I was not available to date someone. I faked my way through that relationship as best I could. I said I was doing great when I was really rotting from the inside out. I couldn't do it anymore.

The relationship lasted till October. I was shocked it went on that long. I will always regret how I broke up with her since it was via text message. But I was going down to Los Angeles to fix my life. Everything else fell by the wayside.

CHAPTER 12
Liars, Cheaters
and Bad Influences

In March of 2010 we went down to Palm Springs for Easter. This was a family tradition and I always enjoyed it. This year was much different. Before the trip there was tension in the family. For some reason, Mom always wanted to move. She'd look at houses all the time and declare that we were moving. My brothers would get excited, and then their hopes were crushed when she let them know that nothing was happening. That March she started looking at homes in San Diego. Zach was really excited and accidentally told my dad. Mom had a real problem with us talking to Dad or sharing anything with him. She would tell us certain things and make us swear to not tell him. She said he would "ruin her and all of our plans." So most of the time we kept secrets from our father. Eventually I would tell him everything. I thought that keeping news from one parent was pointless.

Mom also wouldn't let us talk on the phone with Dad when we were at her house. She said this was her time, and we were not allowed to speak with him on her time. The ramifications of Zach telling Dad that they were perhaps moving to San Diego were brutal. She yelled at him.

"How could you tell your father that? You know what he will do," she said. "What you did is the same as if I went on the loudspeaker at school and announced how shitty your grades are to everyone. How would you feel about that, Zachary?"

My mom's husband continued his ways as well. On the way to Palm Springs, my Mom and I were arguing about something. My stepdad always sided with Mom no matter what the topic. When Mom finally gave up on the argument, he told her, "Consider the source, honey." He degraded me in front of my own mother and called me stupid. What a guy.

That was the prelude to Palm Springs. I was already suffering from depression. Spending a full week with Mom and her husband made it worse.

An argument I will remember for the rest of my life took place halfway through the trip. My aunts, grandma, and Mom were sitting around the table with me. I was telling them how well the Fischler family was doing and that I admired their way of life. They were successful and knew how to get what they wanted. Then all four women bombarded me with their opinions of the Fischlers.

"You do not want to be like any of the Fischler men!"

"They are liars, cheaters and bad influences!"

"I hope you do not follow in any of their footsteps. Your uncles are awful!"

I didn't know how to respond to this verbal onslaught. I was already on the edge and this verbal abuse crushed me. They completely destroyed Dad's family and essentially said they were all awful people.

I left the table in tears and took a walk. My grandma followed me outside. She asked me to sit down with her.

"Why are you crying, Alex?" she said.

"Why do you think I am crying?" I shot back.

"I guess we were a little harsh in there."

"Um, yeah. You think?"

"I am sorry," she said. "I didn't take your feelings into consideration. Looking back on it, my comments were inappropriate. Again, I apologize. That was uncalled for."

She was the only one who apologized to me. None of the other women took responsibility for what they had said.

I was pissed off during the rest of the trip. I was having a terrible time and I just wanted to go home. While I was outside with my grandmother I also shared with her what had taken place between Zach and Mom before we left. She was appalled that Mom would talk to Zach that way.

That night I was hanging out watching television in the rental condo. Mom came in and confronted me.

"Why did you tell your grandma what I said to Zachary?" she screamed. "Do you know how that makes me look?"

I chuckled. I had finally gotten her to admit to some of her ridiculous behavior.

"It makes you look bad," I responded.

The fact that she knew her behavior was unacceptable triggered many questions in my brain. Why did she never admit to any of her other severe lapses in judgment? Did she actually know she acted out this often? Maybe she was not as crazy as I thought. She could just be an awful human being.

These were questions that I wanted answers to. But I knew I never could get straight ones from her.

CHAPTER 13
The Last Straw

ONCE WE GOT BACK TO SAN JOSE I WAS ABLE TO REGROUP. But I let my dad know how close I was to blowing up that trip. A few more of these stupid events and I would be saying goodbye to Mom for a long time.

My mom didn't just abuse my brothers and me. She also demeaned my father in front of us all the time. She told us that Dad was a liar and that he was the reason they were divorced. In addition to that, he had not fought hard enough to keep the marriage intact.

I found out a few years later that the truth was much different. One of my uncles felt like it was time for me to know what had really happened. Dad didn't want him to tell me, but he did anyway. Mom had been sleeping with one of the tenants who lived in the rooming house we moved into. So they both had played roles in the divorce. It was not as one-sided as she had made it out to be.

Besides making fun of my father in front of us, Mom also did this in front of my friends and other families. On a camping trip with family friends she told us that we were lazy like our father. She added that we had gotten this attitude from him and she was tired of it. This was all because we were bitching about doing the dishes.

In hindsight, comments like these were entirely inappropriate. My therapists let me know often that even though I harbor bad feelings for my mom, I shouldn't share them with my brothers. So I rarely ever do. But Mom was always ripping on Dad. Whenever she had the opportunity she jumped on it.

Another example happened at Clear Lake State Park with a good buddy of mine, Michael Sywyk. Michael said he really liked my dad and thought he was funny. Mom immediately shut that down.

"Mr. Fischler is a terrible influence on you boys," she said. "He really sets one of the poorest examples I have ever seen. I have no idea why you would like him, Michael. Alex's dad is just not a good guy. Trust me on this."

Michael didn't know how to respond. He later shared with me how blown away he was that she still felt that way about Dad. It had been almost ten years since the divorce and she was still shitting on him. She acted like the guy she had been married to half of her life was the devil. Truly amazing, if you ask me. I could not hold a grudge for that long. I believe that to this day she is not over it. I also believe that one of the reasons she started to distrust me is because I am became so much like my dad. When I started to play racquetball I think she felt threatened by that too. Her self-esteem is quite fragile.

The trip to Clear Lake happened toward the end of the summer. I was at the end of my rope with mom and her husband. They were not fun to be around, and they treated me like crap. Sure, my basic needs—food, shelter, and things like that—were taken care of. But I had absolutely no emotional support and I never seemed to be able to do anything right in their eyes.

The situation really got out of hand that summer. My

Mom often told me that I was a disappointment to her. I was getting tired of hearing this. I was *not* a disappointment. I would *never* be a disappointment. The only disappointment would be if I never left that house.

The last time Mom called me a disappointment, I gave her a taste of her own medicine.

"What else is new, Mom?"

I was tired of both of their acts and would soon find an opportunity to escape.

CHAPTER 14
Jailbreak

A FEW WEEKS LATER THAT OPPORTUNITY PRESENTED itself. I was my grandma's house hanging out with my brothers. Mom arrived to pick us up but grandma wanted to talk to her. They started chatting about Labor Day weekend. Mom told grandma that she and my stepdad had already made plans: we were going to a family friend's lake house.

I told Mom I didn't want to go. I had other things going on that weekend and could not waste time at a lake house. An argument started, and by the end of it I told her I was done with her. I was leaving her house and that was the end of it. I was tired of all her shit.

I have always believed that being a parent is a privilege, not a right. If you abuse that privilege it should be taken away from you. I was going to take her privilege of being in my life away. She had earned it over the years with all the crap she had put me through.

The car ride back to our house may have been the most intense moment of my life. My mom tried to reason with me.

"Alex," she said, "how could you do this to me? After all I have done for you. I threw you so many birthday parties and let friends come over whenever you wanted. I also got you into Bellarmine. Without me you would have been as successful as you are. I have been a great mother, and this is how you repay me?"

"Yep," I said.

We sat in complete silence all the way back home. I ran into the house and scurried up to my room. I gathered everything that mattered to me. I called my dad and told him to get over to Mom's. I was leaving—for good. This was it.

People may not believe this, but leaving that day was the biggest achievement of my life so far. Having finally mustered up the courage to free myself forever, I left my house key on the kitchen counter and dashed out the door with a few bags across my back.

I was free. I was fucking *free*. For the first time in my life, I was not suffering my mother's wrath. No more emotional abuse. I would never have to deal with her again. I had more control of my life now, and I wanted it to remain that way.

MESSAGES

Hi there,

I thought if you and I focused are energies in a positive way, we might achieve something.

On another note, I would like to invite you and a friend (?) to go with us on Sunday to check out a new boat that Bill [stepfather] and his brother would like to buy. You do know that we sold our boat?

So, the boys want to go too. We are planning to be at Anderson Reservoir Sunday morning at 9:30 a.m. I think we are taking Max kneeboarding and would be able to take others skiing. Michael maybe?

We would really like your opinion on the boat. Figured we would be home by lunchtime. We are planning on bringing it to Lake Almanor next summer. Evidently it's a go with all the McBride [the stepdad's] clan.

My expectation is that we would just get together to talk about what you have been up to, basic updating and what is on the horizon. I would like to see you.

I love you,

Mom

I continued to receive emails like these not long after I left Mom's house. For some reason she thought things were cool and I would be back in no time. I still do understand how she could think that. I had said repeatedly that I was not coming back. I was never going to return. Anyone with half a brain knew that.

These emails bugged me. All I wanted was to be left alone. She did not seem to understand that. I wanted nothing to do with her and she still tried to contact me—an extreme lack of boundaries and respect for her son.

The next email is something my Mom sent to her husband.

Hi,

I wanted to talk with you about how we are going to move forward with the tension created when the boys come back in two days. I really did not like the way you spoke to them and the tone you used with them last week—hence our argument. I will continue to defend the boys until the day I die. Nothing will change that if I feel they are being attacked or spoken to in a way that is offensive. I am about at my wit's end in dealing with this. That is the reason I called us into therapy.

After having heard from Alex's therapist at Kaiser [Permanente, a healthcare provider], the primary reason he is not at the house has to do with his relationship with you. Now we have two kids who have left for generally the same reason, except now I am having one of my children choosing to leave. You will never understand how stressful it is living with someone such as yourself who is so volatile on a daily basis. We never know what kind of mood you are going to be in or what is going to set you off on a mini tantrum. (dog shit on your fingers).

Before even speaking to Alex's therapist, I was considering perhaps whether it would be best to have you home later during the week. Perhaps you might arrive home around 8:00 p.m. I have lost my son over this and it is killing me. I do not want this in my life anymore and you don't seem to recognize the extreme importance of this issue.

Consider being their friend. I don't need you to back me up or discipline the boys. I have asked you if you have a problem with what they are doing to come and talk with me but you continue to take it upon yourself to correct them.

I love you when you are being nice, gentle, considerate, loving and even-tempered. But the person that is present a majority of the time is one that is wearing us all a bit thin.

Loretta

My therapist never said that my stepdad was the main reason I left the home. I called him right after I read the email and he said that was completely false.

In addition, Mom decided to send this email after I left. Where was this email when my stepdad hit Max? Or when he verbally abused us?

The biggest problem I have with this email is she tries to pin everything on my stepdad. She needs to understand that she is and will always be the main reason I will never be a part of that family again. She was the one who abused me the most and she was the one that married him. She created most of the ugliness in that house. She created an environment that was impossible to live in.

I believe my mother is mentally ill. She is incapable of taking any accountability for her actions and does seem to understand the ramifications of her actions. In the past, she has said some of the most horrific and hurtful comments to people. These people in response have either dropped her as a friend or stopped talking to her. She does not seem to know why. Well, Mom, you can't be a bitch to people and expect them to like you. When you hurt somebody, you cannot act like it is water under the bridge. Other people have feelings too.

I hope that one day she will be able to sympathize with others. I was shocked she forwarded this to me. I thought it was completely inappropriate to share the communication between her and her spouse with her son. At one point when I was still living there she asked me if she should divorce him. I had no idea how to respond to a question like that. That is a decision that she should make on her own. There was no reason to involve me in a discussion—again, a real lack of boundaries on her part.

Our relationship was mother-to-son, not friend-to-friend. In life there are certain things you do not talk about with your children. Unfortunately, she often talked about these topics with us.

Once I left the house I received several emails from my Mom begging me to come home.

Alex,

Please note that I have never spoken to your brothers about you coming back here to live. They are so very sad that you are not here and they do not understand why you have chosen not to come home. They do not see things the way you do. I did tell them that it would get better and that

---

eventually things would turn out okay. As I stated in the quote I forwarded to you, you are free.

Please understand that your decision has been made in a vacuum without really thinking through the effect this might have on your brothers. I will be fine. I have had wonderfully happy times with you and will again, but they have only one year left with you being home.

I caught Max in your room last night looking around. I thought he was looking for other items to confiscate, since he has been laying claim to your stuff, but he was very melancholy and said he wanted to be in your room because he missed you.

I know you have taken issue with your perceived limited freedoms here. I never intended for you to feel that way and wish that somehow you could have been more communicative with me rather than appearing obstinate and disrespectful.

If you ask anyone I have spoken to about you, I have often stated that you were [the] happiest being on your own and that I was glad to have raised you to feel comfortable going away to college. I am confident that much of our issues lay in the fact that there has been minimal listening going on.

Alex, I was never intending for you to go with us to the Heatons [family friends of the stepdad's] over Labor Day. You would have been completely bored. Hence the reason I did not have you go with us to San Diego. I did take exception to how you were speaking to me, but I never got the chance to tell you that it didn't much matter to me whether you went with us. I have felt that way about many of our activities lately. I just didn't want you to think I didn't want you with us.

I have always been grateful for the communication we have shared, and I have always enjoyed our conversations. You are a highly intelligent, very thoughtful and introspective young man.

We need to eventually come up with a solution between us to help ease your brothers' concerns, sadness and feelings of loss. I know that with careful consideration of your feelings, we can arrive at a place where your brothers won't feel completely abandoned. I don't know what the answer is yet. Their sadness is more upsetting to me than your absence. Please don't take that the wrong way. Take the space you need, but please remember that there are others involved that are being hurt in the process.

I will always love you. Nothing you can do or say will change that. Let us continue to text one another so that we can keep in touch on each other's happenings.

I hope for nothing but great things for you this year.

Mom

What you just read is a called a guilt trip. This is what my mom does when she tries to cover her ass. Notice that in the email she does not take any responsibility for any of the things she did. She said my limited freedoms were "perceived," meaning she did not think there was anything wrong with the way I was being treated.

This was the first email from her. I received over twenty of these over the past few years. They all say the same thing: I am angry young man who misunderstood everything she put me through. In her eyes, nothing she did was wrong.

CHAPTER 15
Haunted

AFTER I LEFT MY MOM'S HOUSE, MY LIFE TURNED UPSIDE down. I don't think I really understood how much my life was going to change after I made that decision. Like I said I earlier, it was by far the best decision I have made in my life. But all choices have consequences. I cut more than half the people I knew out of my life. There were all friends of my mom, and they were not going to like the choice I'd made.

***

My dad's mother, Bobbie, has always suffered from depression. She is also an alcoholic and a drug addict. I love my grandma, but she has a lot of issues. I feel so bad for her. I hope she realizes that we all are there for her. We want her to get better, but she has to make the changes on her own. Her alcoholism and drug addictions have affected us all.

Bobbie's condition started to affect me personally during a rainy evening in the fall of 2010. I was watching television upstairs and I heard a loud BANG at the base of the stairs. I ran down to see what all the commotion was. I was home alone so I was a little scared. I thought someone had broken in.

It was my grandma. She was holding on to the stair railing. Blood was dripping from her face and she was slurring her speech. I could tell she had taken a combination of drugs and alcohol. I knew that based from the wound on her head she had fallen face-first onto the pavement.

I panicked. I had never seen my grandma in this state before. I ran out the door and jumped into my car. I felt bad abandoning her, but I could not deal with her. I called Dad. He didn't pick up, so I left him a message. He called back a few moments later.

"Alex, what's going on?"

"Grandma is hurt," I said, and explained what I'd just seen.

"Is she okay? Hold on, I'm driving back home now."

When Dad got home we looked for Bobbie. She was not inside the house, so we figured she was out back in the little cottage where she lived.

As we entered the cottage I got an eerie feeling. I thought my grandma was dead. Fortunately I was wrong. We found her lying facedown on her bed, moaning in pain and saying over and over again that her head hurt.

I called 911 and the paramedics arrived ten minutes later. They asked Bobbie a series of questions. *What is your name? What year is it?* She knew what her name was, but she thought that the year was 1952. She was stoned out of her mind.

At first Bobbie resisted care and refused to go to the hospital. We eventually got her to lie on a stretcher. The paramedics loaded her into the ambulance and we headed over to the hospital. I told my Dad I was scared. I was seventeen years old, but seeing my grandma like this freaked me out.

At the hospital, one of the nurses directed us to grandma's room. The room was not well lit and she was lying on one of those hospital beds. She looked as fragile as I had ever seen her.

"Why are you guys here?" she said.

My dad leaned over her. "Mom, you are in the hospital."

She laughed and shook her head. "Get me out of here!"

During the next hour she flashed in and out of consciousness. Eventually the doctor came in and gave us the news: my grandma's alcohol levels were four times over the legal limit.

He looked at her and shook his head.

"Bobbie," he said, "I'm advising you to stop drinking . . . or you'll kill yourself."

Grandma didn't seem to take any of his advice seriously.

One of my first Fourth of Julys in downtown San Jose. Every year the community comes together and celebrates the holiday with a parade through the streets.

Helping Dad blow out the candles of his birthday cake up at my grandparents' house.

A visit to Alcatraz during my senior year of high school. From left to right: Zach, me, Brenda, Max and Dad.

The first year of my soccer career. I would play 'til the end of my 8th grade year.

My favorite baseball season. Hanging out with Daniel and Nick in the dugout before one of our games.

Valentine's day photo shoot with my brothers. I can't believe the photographer got us to stop talking and pose to take this. We are rarely able to take a normal photo.

My first snow experience in Tahoe with my family as a toddler. Dad is helping me get my footing. I just remember it being so slippery and I kept falling.

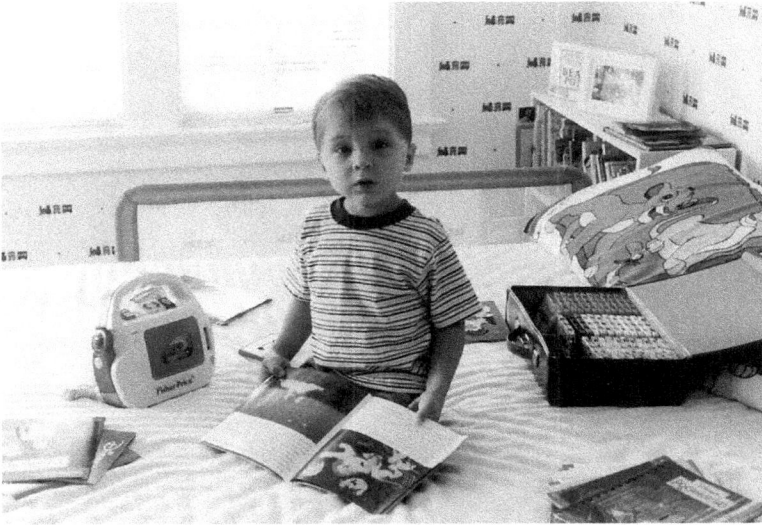

I loved my books and tapes as a child. This was taken in my childhood room while I was deep in a reading session.

Zachary and I having some fun in the hallway. This was a common occurrence before my parents got divorced. Then life took an unpleasant turn.

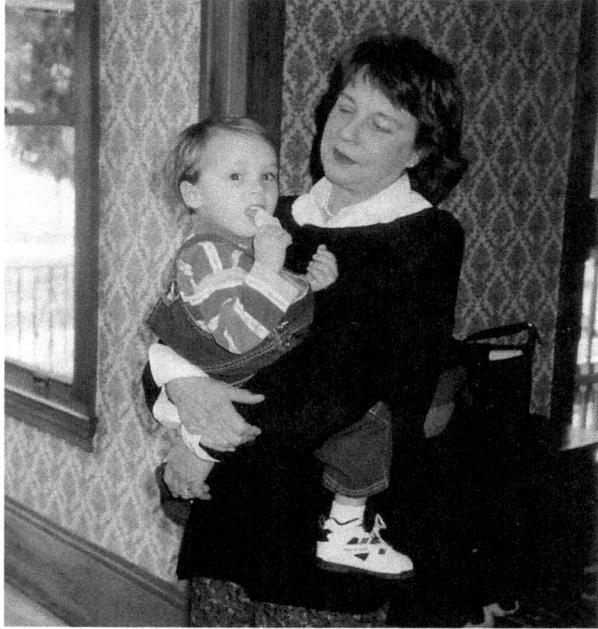

My grandma Bobbie holding me in the dining room of
our childhood home. She looks young and healthy here.
Unfortunately she doesn't come close to this in present day.

My brothers and I help blow out candles on Dad's birthday cake.
Only a year later these types of family celebrations would end.

In our rental house at Bolinas (a small town north of San Francisco) celebrating Max's birthday.

Another one of those photo shoots that bugged the crap out of me. Max, Zach and our cousin Ethan are in this pic. This was a holiday shoot.

Zach and I with characters from *Toy Story* at Disneyland. This was a really fun trip since I was still into getting autographs from all the characters.

My brothers and I in Bolinas at Thanksgiving near the beach.
I remember the wind whipping in our faces during this photo.

Walking back to the mound after throwing a pitch. Before games
I would be so nervous. But once I got on the field my nerves
would settle and all I had to do was throw.

A wallet-sized photo from my first year of soccer. I was excited and ready to play.

Dressing up as Woody one day. I loved putting on costumes as a child. These characters influenced me so much during my youth. They provided an escape from who I really was. I could dress up as them and not have to be myself anymore.

Just looking for something to entertain me in my room as Dad reads the sports page in the background.

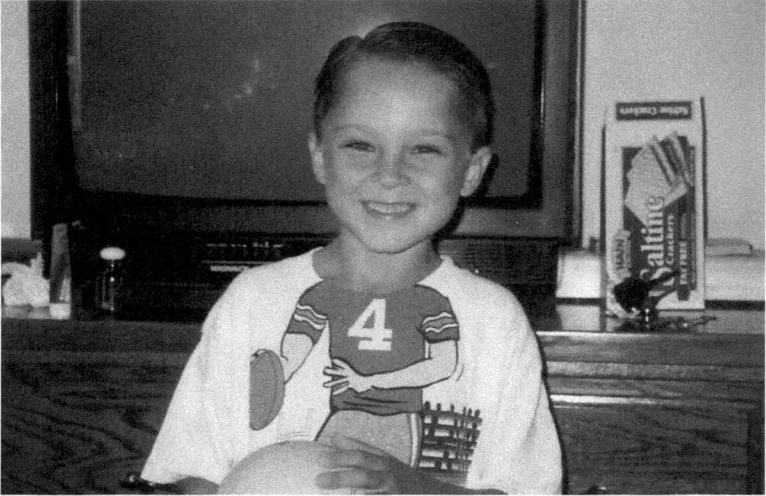

Wearing one of my favorite shirts as a child. It gave me the body of a quarterback. I felt confident in this shirt—like I could always throw the game-winning touchdown pass no matter how much pressure was on me.

Sitting on Mom and Dad's bed, reading one of my favorite childhood books. I was definitely into this particular book since it explained a lot about the animal kingdom.

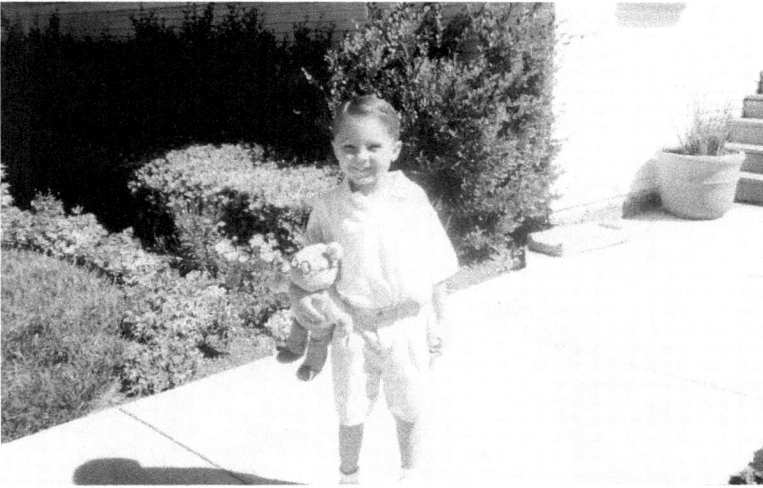

One of my favorite stuffed animals and I in front of my childhood home. I was a happy camper when he was in my arms. I felt a sense of safety and security.

I said early on that I liked Christmas....

Zach and I in another portrait. We look so dapper and handsome. Max had not come into the world yet. So we were missing one of our players.

CHAPTER 16
Breakpoint

CUTTING OFF ALL CONTACT WITH MY MOTHER WAS a tough choice. In some ways it was like ending an unhealthy, abusive relationship. I had to escape my abuser and get on with my life. If I had stayed there is no doubt in my mind that I would have eventually committed suicide. In addition, there is no way I would be where I am today without leaving. I needed freedom in order to accomplish the things I've done in the past several years.

Dad was able to provide me with an environment that encouraged my recovery. He trusted me and wanted me to succeed. My mother always brought me down and blocked my paths to success. My life revolved around making her happy. I couldn't keep living that way.

Dad let me chase my dreams. He trusted me, believed in me and knew I could accomplish everything I set out to do. I cannot thank him enough for his courage during that time. He was getting crap from a lot of people for letting me leave Mom's house. He could have told me to suck it up and stay there. Instead he sacrificed his time and energy toward trying to help me get better. He is one of the main reasons I made it through all of this alive.

I remember some of the discussions we had after I moved into Dad's house full-time. We talked about all the abuse, dysfunction and horrors of living with my mother. Dad had experienced some similar situations when he was married to her. We were able to bond over these experiences, and he began to understand where my depression had originated. He also came in and talked with my therapist once in a while. I could tell Dad cared and was quite worried about me. He had never seen me so sad in my life. I think he knew how important therapy was to my recovery. I needed people—trained professionals in addition to family and friends I trusted—to share my feelings with. There were many different parts to my psyche that had to be healed. Fortunately my team of therapists was able to help on the road to recovery.

***

It was early October and school was stressing me out. My relationship with my girlfriend was not working out, and I was lonely. Dad had a new girlfriend and he was spending a lot of time with her. Her name was Brenda and she was a nice woman. I didn't know much about her, but I knew that she cared about me and it looked like she would be around for the long haul. In the beginning of their relationship Dad had neck surgery. Brenda was there for him every day and helped him recover fully. So I knew she was a good human being. She didn't want kids, so that was a plus, since my dad didn't plan to have more children either.

I was home alone so often that bad thoughts would start to run through my head. I didn't know how to combat the feelings of guilt and depression.

I wonder if anybody would care if I killed myself?
I really have nothing to live for at this point.

I am such a piece of shit and nobody loves me.
Mom was right. I am nothing without her.

I started to cry. I had never been so alone in my life. I was a mentally tough kid, but all of the pain was killing me.

I walked into the kitchen and stared at the knives. I took a knife out of one of the slots. I sat with that knife in my hand for an hour. A few times I ran the knife across my wrist. I felt the metal rub against my veins. Oh, I could end this so quickly. I thought what it would feel like to slice my arm. Just let all the blood leak out and watch myself fade. All of the hurting would be gone. I just needed peace. I longed for a state of calm. I felt like nobody loved me and my life was meaningless.

I put the knife to my wrist. I started to slice the first layer of skin.

As I began to cut, I stopped. I threw the knife on the ground and began to cry.

I thought about my dad. I thought about my brothers. Most importantly, I thought about myself. What would I accomplish by killing myself?

Despite how badly I wanted to die, I could not go through with it. I picked up the phone and called my therapist.

"Alex," he said, "calm down. I am going to get you the help you need. Make it through the night and we'll figure it all out tomorrow."

His voice was reassuring. I trusted him. I knew he genuinely cared about me and would get me out of this mess.

I walked back upstairs and into my room. I lay down on my bed and cried. For the rest of the night I kept crying. I eventually cried myself to sleep.

The next morning I walked into my therapist's office and sat down. He looked at me warmly.

"This is what you are going to do, Alex. I have already talked to your teachers about it. You are going away with your dad for a few days."

"I am?"

"Yes. Just get into the car and go anywhere you want. You have been excused from all your classes for the whole week. Come back in seven days and be ready to start heavy therapy. Oh, and catch up with your classes."

I smiled at him. I thanked him for doing all of this for me. A stranger had never been that nice to me.

I picked up my backpack and walked to my car. I sat in the car for fifteen minutes and thought about what had just happened. I didn't know what to make of all it. I was in such a dark place that the school had excused me from my classes for an entire week. *Wow. They must really care about me.*

I turned the key in the ignition and heard the engine roar. It was time to make some changes in my life.

When I got home, Dad was waiting for me. My counselor had called him ahead of time to tell him what was happening.

"Are you ready to go?" said my dad.

"Yeah. I guess so."

We loaded our bags in the minivan and started to drive. My dad looked at me.

"Alex, where do you want to go?"

CHAPTER 17
A Few Days of Good Feelings

I TRIED TO THINK OF A PLACE THAT WOULD MAKE ME a little happier. Then the word *happier* came to my mind. Then happiest... the happiest place on earth.

"I want to go to Disneyland!" I said.

Dad laughed. "Okay. Let's do it."

We drove for six hours and arrived in Anaheim, California. Most of the hotels had rooms available since it was October, the off-season. I knew the park would be pretty empty too.

After settling in at the hotel my dad asked if I wanted to eat. I told him no. I was tired and ready to go to bed. It had been quite a long day for me.

The next morning we woke up and were off to Disneyland. This trip was probably the most fun I have had in my life. It was just my dad and me.

I went on every ride multiple times. As I had predicted, there was nobody there. The place was a ghost town. I loved it. I felt relaxed and my anxiety started to settle down a little. I was not thinking about home anymore. I was able to get my mind off the horrific things waiting for me back in San Jose.

The day went by quickly. We only visited the Disney park and didn't had time to visit the California Adventure area yet.

I slept for eight hours and was ready to go back to the park. I couldn't remember a time I was so excited to live. I wanted to explore the park and have fun with my dad. I will never be able to explain to anyone how great that week was. I needed that relief so badly.

CHAPTER 18
Interlude

AFTER THE DISNEYLAND TRIP I REALIZED SOMETHING:
I had lost my childhood. After my parents divorced when
I was eight years old, I took on responsibilities that a child
should never have to deal with. Being my mother's emotional
sounding board for nine years had taken its toll on me. I was
unable to have a normal childhood like many of my friends.
I was always stressed out about my mom and her problems.

I believe that is one of the reasons I am so mature for
my age. There is a reason many people have called me an
old soul. I like to think that is a good thing in the long run.

I don't do a lot of the stupid stuff many of the kids my age are doing at this point in their lives. I focus on my goals and try to be as productive as I can, each and every day.

Despite all the positives that come with being that mature, there are drawbacks. I have a tough time connecting with other people my age. I have a very difficult time dealing with women my age. I just cannot seem to understand where they are coming from a lot of the time. They have different goals in their lives and seem to take so much for granted.

Some of the traits I see in my peers bother me. They were rambunctious, annoying, and at times I couldn't bear being around them. They are too much to handle. They have all this energy that I am rarely able to come up with.

This is what my life is. I don't like much of it. But I was dealt those cards and I have to play them the best I can. This is not to say I don't have a good number of friends my age. I am just not a social butterfly like many of the kids my age. I have fewer than twenty photos on Facebook, I do not go to raves, and I rarely party. I'm pretty low-key when it comes to that stuff. I have no desire to smoke weed or do illegal things. That is the way I am and I do not want to change. People can either accept me or reject me. I couldn't care less either way.

CHAPTER 19
Backtrack

When Dad and I got back from Los Angeles and Disneyland there was a good amount of crap waiting for me. I had to catch up on all my schoolwork, I was starting with a new therapist, and there was a huge football game the night I returned.

My therapist warned me that attending the game was probably not a good idea. I was feeling better, but I didn't have a ton of energy. I was very weak and needed more rest. Being the idiot that I was, I went to the game anyway. My best friend was there so I figured I would be okay. Wrong an all accounts. I immediately started to feel sick. I told my friend that I needed to throw up. I ran into the parking lot and barfed my guts out. I felt like I was dying. I probably vomited for a good ten minutes. I sat down against a fence. God, what was happening to me? I had felt so good in L.A. These symptoms must have come on because I was back in San Jose. I guess my stress had returned.

I left the game and drove home. That drive was a scary one. I really had to focus to make it all the way back to the house. My head hurt and my body ached. This was not the best state to drive in. I got home and climbed into bed. I needed to recharge my batteries.

What scared me was this: I had only been in that environment for two hours and I had started to fall apart again.

It was time to meet my new therapist.

CHAPTER 20
Pushing Forward

Monday mornings usually sucked. But this one was different. I was being put into the hands of a therapist who would change my life forever.

When I met her I really liked her. I liked her because her only goal was to help me get better. My other therapists had briefed her on everything I had gone through. She said she had heard of cases like mine, but that mine was very complex. I was going to have to commit myself fully to therapy if I wanted to get better. Seventeen years of damage had to be undone. She was going to hold my hand every step of the way.

I saw her three or four times a week beginning in October of that year. During these sessions we addressed all sorts of problems in my life. We talked about how to improve my future. How was I going to break the patterns of abuse and dysfunction in my family? I would have to be the instrument that created the changes. This meant working hard in and out of therapy. During some sessions she would teach me techniques that helped control my anxiety and how I dealt with my family. Obviously I was not in the best of moods during this time. I was very snappy and tended to mouth off. I discovered that this was a new chip on my shoulder. I could either use it to help myself, or it could destroy me. The choice was mine. Sometimes this chip led to me getting myself in trouble. I lost it at a racquetball tournament in November because my team came two points short of a perfect score. It was safe to say I was overreacting and that I needed to calm down.

Another instance occurred when I was playing racquetball in downtown San Jose. I was playing doubles with my dad and got up in his grill when he missed a few shots. I said some things that I should have kept to myself and really hurt his feelings. My dad even told me a year later that nobody could control me at that time. I was so angry about my childhood and the way I was treated. Unfortunately I was letting this anger leak onto others, especially my brothers. I often yelled at them and demeaned them. When I look back on it, I was a complete asshole. I mean, it was *really* bad.

In addition to therapy, I also began to see a psychiatrist, who prescribed some medication to treat my depression. I started out on Lexapro. Lexapro is an SSRI, a Selective Serotonin Re-uptake Inhibitor. This pill would hopefully balance the chemical levels in my brain and ease my anxiety.

After a few weeks on the medication I didn't feel any different. Except for one, minor, little, thing: I had no sex drive. I could not get or maintain an erection if my life depended on it. I was embarrassed. I called my psychiatrist and asked her what the hell had happened to my penis.

"It's a normal side effect of the medicine," she said. "It should go away in a few weeks."

A few weeks! Boners were a critical part of my life back then. I felt like my dick was broken. I waited a few more weeks, and my psychiatrist turned out to be right. My sex drive was back. In addition, I started to feel better. The combination of therapy and pills was paying off.

To me this was a miracle. I never thought I would get better. It wasn't a complete turnaround, though. I still had sleep issues most nights and had limited amounts of energy. I could rarely play more than three games of racquetball before I became exhausted. It sucked.

I just had to be patient.

MESSAGES

The following email came from my Dad after I lost my temper on the racquetball court with him. I completely embarrassed him in front of his friends. I was really out of control at this point. I was two months removed from Mom's house, and I was carrying a tremendous amount of anger. I used racquetball a stress release.

During this time I put all my anger into the game. I would hit the shit out of the ball and argue every call. I was a madman.

I felt awful after what I said to Dad that day. He did not deserve anything I said to him. We didn't talk for a few days after the incident. I eventually took ownership of my actions and comments. I apologized for my behavior and our relationship was better off for it.

Dad and I have these moments where our relationship is redefined. Sometimes we cross each other's boundaries so we have to take a look in the mirror. Our relationship grows through instances like these.

Alex,

I have been giving more thought to why I am so upset. I think the incident on the court [made me realize] that you really do not have a lot of respect for me. Just the night before, we were discussing love and respect. You made it clear that you can't love someone if you do not respect them. I really feel that your actions toward me on the court were extremely disrespectful. I can't tell you how embarrassing it is to have your son tell you to shut up and threaten to walk off the court in front of two other adults. It is bad enough if we were just by ourselves. It is really awful in front of my peers.

You never hesitate to discount my education, my job and the schools I have attended. Again, very disrespectful and hurtful. I think it is great that you are attending Bellarmine and enjoying it. That doesn't make you better than everyone else. It doesn't mean you are smarter than everyone else.

Yes, you are taking tough classes. That is great for you. Why then do you need to criticize what I have or haven't done? Your words are very hurtful and I am trying to understand why you feel the need to criticize me. I do not believe I have ever claimed to be

the smartest person or the best athlete there is. I know
very well my accomplishments and failures. I am okay with
all of them and certainly do not appreciate you judging me
by them.

Please do me a favor and quit criticizing me. Try to
treat me with respect. This is not the first time I have had to
bring this up with you.

Dad

CHAPTER 21
Trying Something New

AROUND THE SAME TIME I STARTED WITH MY NEW therapist, I received a call from an old friend. Bud Geracie told me there was an opening in the sports department of the *San Jose Mercury News* and that I should interview for it. My therapist encouraged me to take advantage of this opportunity.

I had worked at the *Merc* before, but those were small office jobs. This new possibility was a part-time gig where I would be able to refine my skills as a writer before I went off to college.

The next day I arrived at the *Merc* offices in slacks and a collared shirt. I had nothing to lose. It had been my dream to work there since I was a little boy. Plus, if I got the job, I could start to prove Mom and her husband wrong. They never believed that I could make my dreams come true. The time had come to prove otherwise.

That was the first time that thought had entered my mind. That thought has never left. That thought fuels me on a daily basis. Mom and her husband were not the only people who have doubted me along the way. Each day I am motivated by the thought of shutting their mouths. Nothing is more satisfying than succeeding when others say you cannot.

Most of my coworkers and peers are shocked by how hard I work. But if you know my story, it's not hard to see why. There is so much I still need to do.

***

Once I started the job at the *Mercury News* my life really picked up. I was working about fifteen hours a week, playing racquetball, and taking a few honors/advanced placement courses at school. My time was filled up. My lifestyle had changed. I was all about doing my best in every aspect of my life.

I spent a ton of time reading, learning and trying to understand myself better. I wrote down inspirational quotes to post on my walls in my room. I needed to push myself to my absolute limits if I was going to be successful that year. I was always up finishing homework late, at the *Merc* offices late, or at the gym late. I was being productive for every single hour of the day. I am currently still that way. I see no reason to waste time. There is too much I want to accomplish in life to let time slip away.

CHAPTER 22
Dark Hours

Despite all of the good habits I was putting in place, I was still suffering from depression. It would come and go in waves throughout the week. Some days I would be "on my game" as I liked to call it; other times I would sleepwalk through the day. During weekends I would sleep for ten to twelve hours a night. When I woke up, I was still usually tired. I realized I still hadn't beaten this thing.

In fact, I still haven't beaten it. In one of my recent sessions with my new therapist I expressed my frustration to her. I didn't know the type of Alex that was going to wake up every day.

My therapist answered the question for me in a few ways. One, my Jekyll-and-Hyde existence would continue. That was just part of going through depression. Two, if I stuck to my medication I would eventually stop having these "off days." I knew she was right. I just had to commit myself to the program.

Besides dealing with my own issues, I also had to deal with constant harassment from my mother and her family. My grandparents were begging me to talk to their daughter. My stepdad offered to buy me World Series tickets and a trip to 49ers training camp if I talked to Mom. Antics like these bothered me immensely. I didn't appreciate being baited into talking to her. I would talk to her when I felt the time was right.

Other family members were not the only ones who harassed me. Some of my mother's friends also interjected themselves into the situation. Unfortunately, some of those friends happen to be my buddies' mothers. When I visited my friends I would be reminded about how much I was hurting my mother. I just had to ignore all of this crap. None of those ignorant comments required a response.

One of Mom's co-workers called me six times and texted me five times in one day. I didn't pick up any of the calls or respond to any of the messages. When I walked outside to get something out of my car, there was a note stuck to my windshield. It was from the same woman who tried to contact me earlier.

Finding that note on my car really freaked me out. I was scared. I just wanted to be left alone, and nobody was listening. None of them respected my boundaries or understood where I was coming from. They thought I was a liar and that I was exaggerating the facts.

This harassment continued throughout the year. At one point Mom came to Bellarmine and asked the assistant principal to make me talk to her. The assistant principal said no, of course. Either way, the fact that Mom came to school was inappropriate. She still didn't understand why I wanted to be left alone.

MESSAGES

Before I graduated from high school I went to New York to see if I'd like to attend college there. After I got back, my mom wrote to me:

Hello stranger,

Heard you had a great time in New York. Awesome city, huh?

There are a number of family members that would like to attend your graduation. Please let me know what your current thoughts are on this matter.

Also, you are going to need your clothes for college, so I thought I might box them up and send them over to your dad's. Anything you do not want can be given to Zach or Goodwill.

I would love to see you sometime before you leave for college. Think about it.

I am sending over your Easter gift with the boys.

I love you,

Mom

This was another crossing of my boundaries. A few weeks before I had let it be known that I did not want her at my graduation. Of course she sent me this email. I was angry and essentially told her to fuck off. I did not want her there. She had no right to go. She had not helped get to the point where I was in my life. The people who received an invitation had supported and cared about me.

CHAPTER 23
Graduation

I HAD BEEN GONE FROM MOM'S HOUSE FOR SIX MONTHS but her behavior hadn't changed. The worst of it took place during my high school graduation. I asked my mother and her husband not to attend graduation mass (a Bellarmine tradition) or the ceremony on the following day, a Saturday.

Of course they attended anyway.

I know some people may argue that they had a right to be there since they were my parents. I don't care. When two people abuse you they lose that right. During the mass on Friday, Mom kept glaring at me. Once again, that deep stare that hit me right in the gut and found its way in. I was nervous during the entire mass and thought she would come up to me. That was the last thing I wanted to happen. I also hid from my grandparents and ran off campus to avoid talking to them. I wanted nothing to do with them. Nobody was respecting my boundaries. Graduation day was even worse. A day that was supposed to be full of joy and excitement turned out to be awful. I was completely stressed out. My therapists had set up a designated area for my dad's side of the family to meet me afterward the ceremony. Cops hired by the school also were aware of the situation. The police had an eye on Mom and her husband right when they arrived. There was no way Mom and company would ruin this day for me.

When I first walked out with my classmates I immediately saw my grandparents. My grandpa had a camera in his hand and was videotaping the whole thing. That really put me in an angry mood. I hated being filmed. Then, when I sat down, I looked behind me. There they all were, in the same row. It was comical. They had arrived early to get good seats to watch the graduation of a kid they were slowly killing.

Eventually my name was called. I walked up and received my diploma. As soon as the ceremony was over I found my therapist. She led me to the meeting spot where my dad and friends were waiting. Bud Geracie, Gene Pare, and the rest of the family were there. I felt safe.

The family returned back to our home and celebrated. We discussed my plans for the long run as well as my immediate goals. There was a knock on the door, and my uncle Pete answered it. I recognized the voice immediately: it was my grandmother from my mom's side. She wanted to see me and congratulate me on graduating. Peter knew I didn't want to see her so he told her to go. He took the gift from her and she left.

I was so proud of my uncle. He understood what I wanted, and he followed through. I cannot thank him enough for doing that. His decision not to let her see me was crucial, letting it be known that my boundaries were up and nobody was getting through them. There were a lot of people on my side.

I felt poised and confident the rest of the day. Fortunately I was able to keep it together. We had a nice dinner in Palo Alto. I was officially a high school graduate. I also received a nice poem and letter from my stepmom Brenda. Both the poem and the letter carried the same message:

You have a new start ahead of you, so take advantage of it.
I took these words to heart.

The notes from Brenda were important to me. I finally had a female role model in my life that believed in me and wanted me to succeed. In a few months I would be on my way to New York City for my first year of college.

CHAPTER 24
Los Angeles

THE SUMMER OF 2011 WAS A BUSY ONE. I DIDN'T WANT to spend it in San Jose, for numerous reasons. I decided to move down to Los Angeles and live with my Uncle Pete and Aunt Amy. Amy and Pete have a beautiful home near Santa Monica, and I had a blast that summer.

I wanted to make some money, and Peter offered me a job working construction on one of his real estate projects. Working construction is brutal. I have such an appreciation for what those men and women do now. Digging ditches, tearing apart walls and loading dumpsters is exhausting work.

After my first day of working construction I was exhausted. I woke up the next morning around seven in the morning and had never been so sore. I'd always been an athlete, but my muscles hurt more that morning than after any game or practice in my life. I could barely load the dumpsters that day.

I only lasted three weeks on that job. I wasn't mentally tough enough to do that type of work on a daily basis. The Fischler family has always had a motto: *Don't do something that you can pay someone else to do.* This isn't because we are stuck up or anything like that. We have never enjoyed manual labor. I cannot understand why anyone would. That's just me, though.

My uncle Mike came to the rescue that summer. He was working on a TV show that would air on the Discovery Military Channel. The production company hired me as an intern. At first I had to do all the grunt work. I carried numerous props, brought people food, and took down sets.

I quickly became friends with many of the people on the show. One of those people was Allan Duffin, one of the freelance writers for the show. I always asked him if he needed any help with the scripts. He gave me some film to transcribe and we eventually started talking about ideas for the show. I ended up throwing out some good ideas that

Allan especially liked. Since I had contributed some quality work, the head of production offered me a job as a writer for another show they were working on. Unfortunately, school was right around the corner, so I was only able to work on the second show for a few weeks.

My summer in Los Angeles is one I'll always remember. I met many new people, learned every day, and spent quality time with both of my uncles. I also got to know my aunt Amy much better. I shared my past with her and she was shocked at how well I was doing. Her support and understanding lifted my spirits. Those three months I spent in Los Angeles helped me get back on my feet again.

CHAPTER 25
New York

In September of 2011 I arrived in New York City. I moved into an apartment and was ready to start my new life as a college student.

I decided to go to college back east for a number of reasons. I wanted to get as far away from home as possible. I was fed up with the people in the Bay Area and needed a break. New York presented many opportunities to me. I wanted to go back to my family's roots—we were originally from upstate New York—and understand where I came from.

Relocating to New York at such a young age would turn out to be one of the best choices I ever made. I adjusted to adult life more quickly than friends who went to other colleges.

Unfortunately I never was able to settle in during my time in New York. There was so much going on back home that it distracted me. My dad had his troubles, I was still trying to get back on my feet, and my brothers had a lot going on too.

In addition, Mom and her husband were still harassing me. As soon as I got to New York I started working forty hours a week at a pulic relations firm and taking classes at a local university. Most of my time was split between those two commitments. I didn't feel like a normal college kid. The first semester was a whirlwind. I hung out with many different people and had many experiences. I had a pretty good time.

In October a significant event took place. Mom and her husband wanted to take me off their health insurance. I didn't care, since my dad and I would figure it out one way or another. We always have. Mom said they were going to remove me since I was not part of the family anymore. The only way they would keep me on was if I started talking to Mom again. I thought this was complete crap, so I said no thanks.

The best part about that whole situation was they never took me off the health insurance. They sent me an email saying that they didn't agree with any of my decisions, but family is important so they would keep me on. I laughed to myself. They were making a huge deal out of something I couldn't care less about.

MESSAGES

The following email was sent from Mom's husband in the fall of 2011. They had tried to talk me into speaking to my mother so they would keep me on their health plan. I refused to do that, and this was what I received.

Alex:

I received your email and I don't know where you got the strange notion that this was about bribery. It's about family, Alex. Family is there for one another and has each other's back. Why would anyone pay the insurance for someone with whom they don't have a relationship? I have kept you on the benefits for the past year and have not begrudged it once. But as you make the choice to continue to alienate us from your life, I don't see the point of continuing this.

I will say this again... We love you. We want you in our lives and we want to continue to have you on the benefits. But... it's a two-way street. Please know

---

that when I take you off, it will be very difficult to ever reinstate you. My hope is that you will have a change of heart.

I was quite busy during the fall. In my spare time I went to the gym. I needed to stay in shape. Dad and grandma Bobbie had got me a membership at the New York Health and Racquet Club. This place was pretty cool. It was located right across the street from the Staten Island ferry. The weight room had a great view of the East River. The club also had two racquetball courts. Every Wednesday I would go and play with the guys there. The competition was solid and I always got in a good workout.

***

One of the most interesting parts of living in New York was having two gay roommates. This was not by choice. I have nothing against gay people. But living with two gay men was quite an adventure. It is safe to say that after living with them I can survive any living situation thrown at me. The guys often brought their friends over, which was awful. They would drink all the time and wake me up every night. Hey, some people had to work the next day! They never seemed to understand that concept.

Our relationship was not the best. They thought I was a stuck-up prick who wanted nothing to do with them.

I honestly don't know where they got this notion since I rarely spoke to them. The whole situation was bizarre.

The only good part of my living situation occurred when they invited girls to our place. The girls would take their clothes off in front of me because they thought I was gay too. So that was a plus. I saw probably five or six naked girls in my room during the spring semester. They would change right in front of me before they went out to nightclubs. Those moments will always be imprinted in my memory . . . and will always bring a smile to my face.

I didn't date when I lived in New York. I was too busy with my work, and I figured that girls were too big of a distraction. I had a casual fling here and there but that was all.

***

When I went home for Christmas break my life seemed to be at peace. However, the rest of my family was having a difficult time. Dad was still suffering from the accusations from the girls at Holy Spirit school. My brothers Zach and Max were struggling in school and seemed to be a little confused about things in general. There was not a lot of happy when I came home.

My grandmother Bobbie was no longer living in her own house. Dad had checked her into a rehab facility in Los Gatos. She had started to lose track of time and was living in a drunken haze. She was forgetting basic details and sleeping all day long.

I spent most of my Christmas break at Bobbie's rehab facility. They were cleansing her. She had no access to alcohol or cigarettes. "Being cold turkey is killing me," she said.

When it was over and we would ask Bobbie about her stint in rehab, she remembered none of it. She was so drugged out at the time, she didn't know who we were. I must admit it was pretty crazy. Grandma constantly demanded to return home. My Dad told her no. He was not going to let her come back. He didn't want her alcoholism and drug addiction near my two younger brothers. He had dealt with enough of it when he was a child. He refused to put his own children through it. Bobbie argued, but Dad wouldn't budge.

During the holidays we found a new home for my grandma. It was a facility for the elderly, where she'd have her own apartment. We could move all of her furniture in.

I am happy to say that my grandma is still alive. She is living in Willow Glen, a community in San Jose, and seems to be enjoying herself. This has been one of the few bright spots for our family over the past several years.

Both sides of my family have a history of drug and alcohol problems. I am Irish and German. Therefore Jameson's Irish Whiskey might as well run through my blood. My grandma is just one example of a family member who struggled with addiction. Her behavior had a big impact on me. I saw what taking all those pills and drinking excessively could do to a person. I didn't want to be like her. Don't get me wrong: the woman is brilliant. She was accepted to Cal State Berkeley when she was just sixteen years old, and she ran the local League of Women Voters in San Jose for many years. But she has at least as many demons as I have. She is haunted, and my heart goes out to her.

MESSAGES

While I was in New York, my Mom sent me this email about Bill, her husband.

Hi Alex,

I hope your weekend was better than mine. Bill was rear-ended on the Sunol grade and his car was totaled. Thankfully Bill is okay, but we now need to find a new car for him. Zachary is pretty excited about that. And one of my new kitties was killed by a car last night. Diane found him this morning. It was a really sad day, and his sister Gracie is showing signs of grief. I hope she perks up soon.

I don't know if the boys told you that Lady has cancer of the spleen. I am trying to feed her nutritious food every day, but she is getting pickier and pickier. She is just skin and bones these days. Work is great, however. It has been fun working with Sarah [a friend] again. She is always such a hoot.

I have heard that you will not be coming home for Thanksgiving. I know you will probably think I am totally absurd for offering this, but I have the entire week off and would be thrilled to come out and visit and see where you are living. It breaks my heart that you may be alone on Thanksgiving, so I wanted you to know that if you are inclined to talk and resolve the issues between us, I would not hesitate to fly out there. The same goes for Easter. I do not know what your schedule is, but we are all vacationing in Palm Springs again for a week and I would be more than happy to fly you directly there to join us all.

I am well aware of the fact that you are still very angry with me, but I will share something with you that a wise person told me recently. What you focus on becomes your reality. And if you want to continue focusing on having a bad mother, that is all you will ever have. But it is your choice how you hold events, situations and feelings in your conscious mind. My choice is to hold all the great times we had together in my consciousness as my reality. You have hurt me pretty badly with some of the things that you have said and done, Alex. There are two sides to every story. But I don't want to live my life with that as my focus. I miss you so much and all our great conversations, great trips, great birthday parties and fun activities together.

I love you Alex and we forgive people because we want to have our son, daughter, mother or father in our lives. Please forgive me. I will forever be here for you with open arms. You are my son and nothing will ever change that or the undying love I will have for you until I die.

Mom

This is another guilt trip. Paragraph one consists of several tragedies in her life that I should empathize with. She wants me to feel bad for her so I will start talking to her. I should not feel overwhelming sorrow for you because your cat died or your husband crashed his car. None of that has anything to do with me. The middle is the best part. Yes, I do think you are absurd for offering to visit me during Thanksgiving. The last person I want to spend a holiday with is you, the woman who terrorized me for so many years. Some of what I just said may come off as selfish and asshole-ish. When your mother takes your self-esteem and smashes it, let me know. The aftermath is remarks like these.

I don't care what is going on in her life. I don't want to be a part of her life. None of it is relevant to me. I have my own life and problems. She does not need to throw her issues on to me. This is what she did throughout my childhood. I am done being the sounding board. The ten-year-old took care of the forty-year-old far too many times.

Dear Alex,

I have spoken to a myriad of people and have heard so many different reasons to as why we are having this estrangement. I am not sure where the truth lies, but I did want to say that I am sorry.

I have been told that your relationship with your stepdad was too stressful and that you felt that I did not come to your defense often enough. I am sorry if you felt that way because you have always been my priority.

I am also aware that you felt that you could not have the freedoms that you needed here and I wish that I had been a better listener.

I know that I do not trust easily and that this is a holdover from growing up with a mother who overreacted to everything so that I could not trust her to be reasonable about anything. Nor did she ever take anything I had to say seriously. I have really not tried to be that dramatic mother, and one that was consistent enough in her reactions that I was also reliable. There have been very few people I have trusted that have not broken my trust at one time or another. Your occasional lying made me question the words that came out of your mouth. I am hopeful that in time we will build a relationship based on trust.

I know that I have done some things that have really angered and hurt you. I cannot take those things back. But please know that every relationship, given time, will have situations that require a great deal of forgiveness. Please forgive me.

I would like to be able to see you soon and have a conversation. I would really appreciate being a part of your senior year because it holds such exciting things, and I want to share those with you.

Please let me know how we can proceed to repair our relationship. It is one of the most important to me and as I have said before, I have missed our conversations.

Love,

Mom

This is written by someone who will do whatever it takes to get her way. My mother wrote this because she wanted to show everyone that she was trying her best to get me back. In none of these letters does she take responsibility for her behavior. She just apologizes for things that may have angered me.

Let's start with the first paragraph. She had no business going around asking people why I had left. That shows a complete lack of respect for me. Do some self-reflection and you will find the answer. All the other people do not know why I left. Deep inside she knows why. Once again, my relationship with my stepdad was not the reason I left. The reason was because of my relationship with you—a relationship so broken that not even a therapist could fix it.

In terms of being a dramatic mother she has excelled. Every day was like a tragedy. I often saw crying, passive-aggressive behavior and verbal abuse. If that does not exemplify self-created drama then I have no idea what does.

I lied to her to escape her unrelenting wrath. Everything I did either pissed her off or made her cry. It was a lose-lose situation each day. I could do nothing right in her eyes. Therefore I started to lie to protect myself. I could not handle living with her anymore.

I will not forgive her. This apology should have come at least two years prior.

CHAPTER 26
Changing My Mind

AFTER TWO WEEKS IN SAN JOSE I WAS READY TO GET BACK to New York. I was feeling good in January of 2012 when I returned back East. I felt like it was time to get off my antidepressants. I also decided that I wanted to transfer schools. The college I was at in New York was not meeting my needs and I wanted real college experience—a college that included an actual campus, a rec center and a real sense of community. I knew when I was older I would move back east. But at this point in my life New York was not the place for me.

I searched for a new university that had a good journalism school and a racquetball team. Those were my only criteria. I didn't care where the school was located. I found the University of Missouri, also known as "Mizzou." I applied and waited to hear my fate. I had earned a high grade point average in New York, so I wasn't too worried.

I got in! I was excited. I was going to a school that had a racquetball team. How cool was that? Plus they had one of the best journalism schools in the nation. Sure, the school was in the middle of nowhere, but that made no difference to me.

At the time I had no therapist and started to slowly wean myself off of the medication. Bad idea. I had no clue about how this would affect my last two months in New York. In March I fell into a deep depression. I spent many hours of the day sleeping and longing for home. I felt as bad as when I'd first left Mom's house. My batteries were low and I could only manage two to three tasks a day. I attended class, went to work, and hit the gym. That was all I did in March and April.

I gutted it out as hard as I could and eventually was on a plane back to California. I had survived my time in New York and was looking forward to a fresh start in Missouri.

Don't get me wrong: I loved New York. I still am in love with it. The city is so magical. I have always been attracted to the lights of New York. If I have the means I will probably return once I graduate from Mizzou. New York is where my roots are. In my blood I am a New Yorker; I know it and so do my friends.

***

I arrived at the University of Missouri in early August of 2012. I didn't know what to expect. The last time I'd been in the state was during a family reunion when I was twelve or thirteen years old.

Dad booked the weirdest flight path ever. We had three different plane changes and didn't arrive into St. Louis till 5 p.m. After picking up our bags we took a shuttle to the rental car center. Dad had reserved a nice little four-door car, and we were off. Columbia, Missouri, is located pretty much in the center of the state, equidistant from Kansas City and St. Louis. The drive out there took a long time, and there wasn't much to look at between St. Louis and Columbia. Fields and crops surrounded us on either side.

I took a nap and Dad woke me up when we were close.

I called my soon-to-be roommate David Faron. He gave us directions on how to find my new place once we hit the Columbia city limits.

The long day of traveling was finally over. Dad and I pulled up to the Copper Beech complexes on Old Highway 63 South. The apartments looked as nice as they did on the university's Web site. I really liked what I saw. My place was all the way in the back of the complex.

Then I met my roommate. David Faron opened the door and strolled on out. I was pretty stunned when I met him. He was one of biggest guys I had ever seen. He had to be taking some sort of steroids to get that big! The funny thing about David is that if you don't know him, he probably scares the shit out of you. His arms are the size of cannons and he struts around like nobody can touch him. In reality, though, he is one of the nicest guys out there.

Once I got all my stuff moved in, Dad and I drove around the town. We eventually hit up Kohl's department store so I could purchase some bedding and other necessities. We ate in a burger joint across the street. After checking out the town, we returned to my apartment. Dad would stay in Columbia for a few days and then head back home.

I was shocked at how many college kids were already in

town. They were everywhere—at Kohl's, at the burger place, at my complex, all over. This was going to be much different than my first year at college. Columbia was the complete opposite of New York. New York is a million times larger. In Columbia the pace of life was slow. But I really appreciated that. I had the peace and quiet I needed to do my work. Living there also lessened my anxiety. There was much less stress here than in other places I had lived.

The next morning Dad wanted to work out. So we went to the university's rec center. Little did I know, this rec center had been ranked the best in the country. I was in awe of how big these facilities were. *Four* glass racquetball courts? *Two* state-of-the-art weight rooms? Fifty different types of workout machines? This was heaven. There was no reason for me to be out of shape while going to school there. Everything I needed was right there for me. I was excited to get to work.

My goals for my first year at Mizzou were pretty straightforward:

Get solid grades
Get another job
Make the racquetball team
Try to be a little more social
Enjoy myself

I thought these were pretty plausible goals. Once school started I became very busy. My classes were easy, but getting the hang of a different lifestyle was hard. This was the third part of the country I had lived in the last three years: West Coast, East Coast and now the Midwest.

I was little weary when the school year began. The energy I had when I first arrived started to vanish. I was in a new state, trying to make new friends and to fit in the best I could. I didn't have a car, so I took the Copper Beech shuttle to class every day. That began to bother me. This shuttle had no air conditioning. It was hot and muggy on the bus, especially during the afternoon.

My first two weekends at Mizzou kind of sucked. I was not yet twenty-one so I couldn't go to any of the bars with my roommates. I spent my evenings writing and watching movies and TV shows on Netflix, the Web streaming service.

After that second weekend I was dying for racquetball to start. Our first practice was fun. I met a few of the guys and started to get the cobwebs out of my system. After playing with a few of them I knew I could make the team. I just needed to work on a few different areas and I would be fine.

That same week David had an idea: he'd find someone who looked like me so we could use his ID to get me into the bar.

David kept trying to think of someone he knew who looked like me. "Dude!" he said. "You know who looks like you? *Alex!*"

To clear up any confusion, Alex was our other roommate. They decided to call me Al when I moved in. I didn't like the nickname, but it could have been worse.

The next day Alex went to the DMV and picked up an extra ID. That Friday I would go out with them. I was excited. They liked me enough that they wanted me to hit the bars with them. This was going to be fun.

Friday night arrived. Around 9:30 we went out on the deck and smoked cigars. Well, David and Alex smoked cigars. I smoked a cigarillo—I couldn't handle one of those big cigars. Brad, one of David's friends, came over. Brad's brother worked at one of the local clubs, so there would not be a problem getting me in. I felt like this was all pretty risky, but I trusted David.

An hour later we finished our cigars and went back inside. All of us got cleaned up. After showering and getting dressed, I came downstairs. David was waiting with a big smile on his face.

"You are going to grow up this year, Al!"

I laughed to myself and figured, *What the hell?* I needed to have some fun anyway.

A few minutes later we jumped in the car. Yes, I know, this was essentially drunk driving since David was a little tipsy. But I don't need to hear a lecture right now from anyone. I am alive at the moment so that is all that matters.

David pumped some music in the car, hit the gas, and a few moments later we pulled into a parking lot. The club we were going to was called Ten Below. Brad's brother met us at the front door and helped us cut through the line. We were in!

By the time I got home that night, I was exhausted. I had fun though, and that was important to me. The best part about that night? It wasn't what I like to call "stupid fun," like when morons my age say "YOLO!" (you only live once) and jump off a bridge to their deaths. What we did was pretty contained, and I saw nothing wrong with it. I woke up the next morning with a smile on my face. It had been worth it.

The next few weekends were more of the same. We went out every weekend and had a blast. This was one of the first times I had gone out and really enjoyed it. My closest friends know that I tend to be a very private person. I rarely ever go out with others. But this was different. I was with my roommates and we were enjoying ourselves.

Between these fun outings and racquetball tournaments the first semester flew by. Before I knew it I was home for Christmas break.

MESSAGES

Hi Alex,

I sure wish you would be open to some sort of discussion. This painful estrangement is not good for so many of us in the family, and you are so attached to what happened two years ago that I fear it is unhealthy for you. I feel so bad about the heavy amounts of pain that obviously still haunt you. Things could be so much better for you and me if you chose love instead of hate.

I think about you everyday and pray that you will have a change of heart.

I love you more than life itself,
Mom

P.S. Please know that I would love to send you money or whatever else you may need while you are away at school. Missouri is a great journalism school, and the campus is beautiful. I am sure that you are going to have a great experience. Be safe and Godspeed.

Hi Alex,

I hope your semester is going well. I am sorry I have been so remiss in telling you congratulations on your success at the racquetball tournament. I am so proud of you and wish that I could have been there to see you play.

We were just in Palm Springs enjoying the beautiful weather. I grow more concerned about Melmo. She appears weaker every time I see her. She was doing so much better when she could attend her Parkinson's classes up here at the Villages. She has left her support system, and she seems to regret having left. It is hard to watch your mom deteriorate so quickly. I hope she finds peace in the desert.

I have a birthday card for you along with a monetary gift. I would love it if you would give me your address so that I could just send you these things via snail mail. I promise that I would not abuse it.

I love you always,
Mom

CHAPTER 27
Holiday Dinner

CHRISTMAS BREAK OF 2012 MAY HAVE BEEN THE MOST FUN I have ever had. One of my best friends was having parties every night at his house. There was alcohol, weed and more. At times it was pretty insane. We would sleep all day and party all night. None of us had work so there was nothing else to do. The beer pong games were epic and there were girls left and right. When I was not at his house I spent time with my family and playing racquetball.

The craziest moment of my year may have come during Christmas dinner with my family. When the Fischler family gets together, things always get heated. Egos are thrown around left and right. My dad and uncles will banter back and forth for hours. They are hilarious.

I'll remember that evening for the rest of my life. Everyone in my family was at the table. Someone brought up the topic of Dad's exes. This is a subject that Dad is very sensitive about. He hates it when people bring up his ex-wives. Uncle Peter decided this was the perfect time to talk about all of them. He called Leslie "an embarrassment to the family" and the blonde "a porn star." I think many of the people at the table were stunned. I, on the other hand, was not. This was coming from the guy who will stoop to any level at any time. He pulled pranks all the time, like throwing rocks at my window to wake me up on Christmas morning, or spilling popcorn on our living room carpet and blaming it on me.

I laughed at these remarks because I couldn't believe he was so idiotic to say them. I laughed so hard I had to excuse myself. Dad was so offended that he went off on Uncle Peter. The rest of the night was pretty ugly. Dad was not in the mood for fun, and my brothers kept arguing for no good reason.

***

Merry Christmas. . . .

Christmas morning was low-key, as it always had been at the Fischler home. We are not huge holiday people and try to get through all of it as quickly as we can. After opening gifts at Dad's house, my brothers headed over to Mom's to open their other gifts. The rest of us stayed at Dad's and hung out. We went and saw a movie later . . . and Christmas was over. The day went smoothly and I was glad I got through it.

Previous to this, the holidays were nightmares. They brought a lot of unwanted stress into my life because they were opportunities for Mom to try and pull stunts, whether it was sending over baked goods or buying me gifts. I didn't appreciate her efforts. I told her repeatedly not to send me gifts. She continued to cross those boundaries, which was disappointing to me. I think that is symbolic of the amount of respect she has for me.

CHAPTER 28
Comeback

THIS PORTION OF THE BOOK IS DEDICATED TO self-improvement. I wanted to write a guide to help people understand that they can indeed beat depression. They can get past the ugly times and bounce back. During the next few chapters I will take you through the exercises and tools that helped me when I was down.

Depression

I always find discussions about depression intriguing. How can someone feel so low that he or she would want to take their own life? I realized it was much easier than I had ever imagined.

When I was fighting depression and anxiety, my body started to break down. I thought my mind was the only victim of these awful conditions. As it turned out, my depression attacked *every* system in my body. I weighed as little as 125 pounds at one point. I had no appetite, vomited often, and my body ached. When I did eat, I stuck to soup or something light. My body couldn't handle meat, bread or dairy products. I knew I was sick, but I never really understood how bad it had gotten. I had no body fat. I could clearly see my ribs in the mirror, and there were always dark rings around my eyes. I was also pale and anxiety-ridden. I shook all the time. My therapists told me I looked like a walking corpse. I hope to God I never feel that way again in my life. I was so frail, lifeless and was headed for death.

My depression was the result of stress, low self-esteem and loneliness. The stress was caused by my being my mother's emotional sounding board and dealing with her shit on a daily basis. She was a control freak and would not leave me alone. I also dealt with pressure from her husband. He was a monster at times when I lived with them. Some of the comments he directed towards me were hurtful and damaging.

I think that people often don't understand how much weight their words carry, especially in relationships between parents and their children. In my case, I looked to my parents for unconditional support and love. At Mom's house I received neither of those. In fact, I received the opposite. The love and support was only given to me if I did what she wanted. If I didn't submit to her requests, I was looked down upon and alienated. This led to a drop in my self-esteem.

I had always been a confident kid. I was a good athlete, student and human being. At least this is what I thought I was, for a while. But the way I was treated by my mother and stepfather completely shrunk me. They often told me that I would never be able to accomplish my goals. Mom repeatedly said that I could not go to college on the East Coast. She said I would not like it there and that I wouldn't survive. Both she and my stepdad tried to define how my life would play out. They made fun of my dreams for the future, and their behavior sickened me.

I knew the main reason they said these things was because their own self-esteem was low. My mother was a teacher but had never been satisfied with what her life had become. She always wanted a better place to live, better material goods, and she was never happy. Her husband attended college late in life. His son had stopped talking to him and most of the people in our family didn't like him. He was a complete asshole. He treated my brothers and me like shit and everybody knew it. So his hateful words toward me came from a place of hurt and torment. But understanding their pain doesn't excuse their actions. They were fully grown adults who needed to be held accountable for their behavior.

My self-esteem was in the gutter, and I had to find a way to pump it back up. I was lonely too, for several reasons. One, I'm not a very outgoing person. I like having friends, but I'm not a social butterfly. Therefore, there were not many people I could talk to about what was happening at home. Nor could I share my feelings with my grandparents, since they sucked down my mother's bullshit juice like it was a milkshake.

All of the feelings I had inside made me feel different than everyone else my age. I felt old and weary. My friends were full of energy and passion. I was envious; I wanted some of that. I had to find a way to get my swagger back. I was able to do that through therapy. But therapy only provided an outline for what I needed to do. Most of the improvement occurred *between* therapy sessions. I did a lot of self-work and reflection. I tried to better myself in every aspect of my life.

So how do you get yourself out of hell? "Hell" meaning a depression-riddled life with no hope, a life where no one and nothing can make you happy? Well, here's how I did it. Take these suggestions at face value. What worked for me may not work for others. These tips can be applied for bouncing back from any difficult situation. I think most of them form the basic structure of a quality called resiliency.

1. Find a therapist.

I cannot emphasize this enough. Many people think therapy is a joke. Trust me, it is the farthest thing from one. My therapists are the reason I am here today. Without them I would be dead. I find therapists helpful because they listen to you and assess your situations with no biases. They will tell you if what you're doing is right or wrong, and they are on nobody's side. All they truly care about is your well-being.

Another reason my therapy was so crucial was because my team of therapists provided a support system. I could call them anytime and they were ready to help.

I advise getting a therapist even if you are not suffering from depression or other symptoms. You can tell them anything you want, and it is always between you and them. I told my therapists things that nobody will ever know. Doctor-patient confidentiality is a great concept, in my opinion. My dad would never hear anything from my therapists unless I was thinking of hurting myself. So in therapy I could discuss the problems with I had with my dad, and learn to deal with them in a healthier way.

I have nothing but good things to say about therapy. I'm happy to say I am in still in touch with all of my therapists and continue to consult with them on personal issues. They are my team and I would not be where I am without all of their help.

2. Get on medication.

This really only applies to those who are suffering from depression, anxiety, and similar issues. The usefulness of effective medication cannot be understated. It was important in my case because the chemicals in my brain were not balanced.

The medications that my psychiatrists prescribed worked miracles. The drugs have lifted my mood, eased my anxiety, and given me the energy to live a productive life. My friends always ask if there are side effects or if the meds make me feel weird. Usually during the first two weeks of being on the medications I experienced some side effects. But they tended to go away pretty quickly.

How did the medications make me feel? I have only felt better when being on them. When I was off my medication, my energy levels dropped and I started to feel awful. My mental state was a mess and I didn't want to be alive. That is how crucial my medication is to me. I have taken two different types of anti-depressants, both of which have worked well. In addition to those I take anti-anxiety and sleeping aid pills. This trio has completely turned my life around.

Once you get into therapy, I highly recommend asking about medication. But here is my warning: only taking pills will not get you to where you want to be. The combination of medication and therapy are dynamic. One really does not work as well without the other, in my opinion.

3. Find some inspiration.

When I felt suicidal I felt like there was nothing to live for. I needed to find a source of inspiration to give me a kick in the ass. Those sources were the music of Michael Jackson, getting good grades, and winning in racquetball.

I first started listening to Michael Jackson's music when

I was a little kid. I was a huge fan and used to dance to his music videos. When he passed away in 2009, my admiration for his art grew. I read his autobiography and highlighted every passage that made an impact on me. I also read through the lyrics of all his songs and wrote down the lines that I connected with. Once going through all of this, I realized that he and I had a lot in common. We both had lost our childhoods, suffered from similar issues, and were perfectionists.

Listening to his music comforted me in my darkest times. To this day I still have a journal full of notes from all the research I completed on his work. In fact, I even have a tattoo on my right shoulder with some of his lyrics: *I am starting with the man in the mirror . . . and no message could have been any clearer.* The song "Man in the Mirror" has always meant a lot to me. The melody and the words come together to create a message with great impact.

When I get up in the morning I am always looking at the man in the mirror. I ask myself, *What can I do to make this world a better place?* I remind myself how lucky I am to be in the position that I am in. I need to take advantage of this opportunity and push myself, to train and cultivate my talents to the highest level possible. As you can tell, Michael Jackson has had a tremendous influence on me.

Getting good grades and winning in racquetball were always goals of mine. Once I left my Mom's house I achieved the best GPA of my academic career, and I'm now an All-American racquetball player.

Earning a higher GPA inspired me for a few reasons. First, I knew I could do a lot better than I had during my first three years in high school. I was being given the opportunity to focus solely on my schoolwork. In the past I was distracted by the issues going on within my family. I wanted to prove that I was as smart as people said I was. On my junior year report card a few teachers wrote that I didn't put in enough effort in their courses. This ticked me off because I knew it had a direct correlation to my depression. As the depression got worse, my grades started to slip. My teachers' comments ignited a fire in me. I wanted to show that I could put in the work that was needed to earn an A.

Winning in racquetball was important to me because I am one of the most competitive people out there. I hate to lose, especially when it comes to sports. I decided that I would put all of my effort into becoming a better player. I went to the gym every day and worked my butt off. I played racquetball every afternoon. My days consisted of school from 8 a.m. to 2:40 p.m., racquetball from 4 to 6 p.m., and work from 7 to 11 or 12 p.m. depending on the night. This daily structure was important in my recovery. I was able to find some solid ground and keep myself occupied.

4. Spend time with family and friends.

I've never been a very social person. But I couldn't have gotten through my dark times without the help of my family and friends. My dad has been amazing through all of this. He has had my back and never doubted any of my decisions. Knowing that I have such strong support from him has meant the world to me. He has loved me unconditionally and I cannot thank him enough.

My friends were also unbelievable during this time. Most of them don't know the whole story of what I've gone through, but they understood that my life was upside down. They invited me over often and were always willing to talk when I needed it.

My best advice is this: do not isolate when you are feeling down. Surround yourself with the ones who love you. One of my therapists calls these people the ones who "feed your soul and spirit." They make you a better human being and give you the will to live. These people lifted my mood and always made me feel better.

The first summer I came home from college they all helped me. We were always hanging out together and having a good time. Whether that meant driving around San Jose, going up to San Francisco, or chilling at home, I kept busy. These outings with my buddies and my family aided my recovery. They created bonds that can never be broken.

5. Stay busy and keep your side of the street clean.

There are two different components to this piece of advice. Staying busy is important for numerous reasons. One of them is because it allows your mind to relax. When I was in deep into depression, all I had were bad thoughts. I would think about all the bad things that happened in my past. This wasn't good for me. Once I got a job and committed myself to school there was less time for my mind to wander through the past. I was involved in so many different activities and groups that I was exhausted by the time I got home. I would fall asleep quickly instead of getting lost inside my head.

In terms of keeping your side of the street clean, this is simple. When you are working toward your goals, a lot of good is going to come your way—that is, if you commit yourself fully. Once all this good is in your life, do whatever you can not to give it away. You will feel a certain high, almost like you are untouchable. Try not to act on this high. I guarantee that you may get yourself into trouble. You will feel invincible and therefore do something stupid. Think before you act.

6. Write down your goals.

Once I established clear objectives for myself, life became a lot clearer to me. I knew where I wanted to go and what I needed to do to get there. I wrote my goals on a piece of paper and taped them to my mirror, so I could be reminded of them every day.

Here in Missouri I do the same thing. I have a white board with inspirational quotes written on it, and I have five pieces of paper taped to my mirror. I think that having goals is extremely important. I believe life is not worth living unless you have them.

Your goals can be anything you want them to be. Just remember, do not overreach. Start out slowly and give yourself realistic goals. My goals early on were simple: do well in school and racquetball, enjoy myself, and study great artists. All of that was plausible and attainable.

Now my goals are much different. I want to write more books, win a national racquetball title, and be kind to everyone I meet. As you can see, your goals will change and develop as you grow.

7. Don't take what others have to say so seriously.

Everyone who knows me will tell you that I don't care what others think of me. I never have and never will. I see no reason to waste time and energy caring about another person's opinion of me. There are too many people I know who try to change themselves to fit in with others. I find that absolutely ridiculous. For a long time I heard only criticism or other harsh talk about me. If I had listened to what those people said about me, I would have committed suicide by now. It is really that simple. So don't listen to them. Instead, listen to the people who support you and want you to succeed. They are the ones who will help build up your self-esteem.

Another important issue is not listening to what others want you to do. I'm talking about people who tell you what you *should* do or what your goals *should* be. That is complete bullshit. *You* control your life. You make your own goals and decisions. Don't let other people take that away from you.

You own your goals and dreams. Never let someone else hinder or change those. If you do, you will regret it.

8. Believe in yourself.

Yes, I know this line is overused. But I mean this in every sense. Not enough people believe in what they have. Realize that you are a talented human being and have a bright future. I can say this about everyone I know. We are all gifted in one way or another. Each of us has special God-given talents. If you don't find yourself with some special skills, then hard work has also been known to accomplish a lot in the world.

This is what kept me alive. I knew that one day I would be able to blossom. I just had to fight off all the bad thoughts and emotions. If you are able to recognize your talents and gifts, you are in business. This leads to hope. Hope leads to believing in the process and in yourself. By "the process" I mean the road to getting back to where you once were, to the person you really are. For me this meant living a meaningful life, enjoying my friends and family, and being successful. That is what I craved to get back to. I knew I could get there. I just had to be patient.

9. Get back to the basics.

We all have personal routines and practices that lead to success. These steps are different for everyone depending on their own life experiences. My basics have always revolved around one simple sentence: *Put in the work and the results will come.* If I put all I have into each facet of my life, it will all work out. Whether it be school, sports, work or relationships, this philosophy has never failed me.

10. You have to do it yourself.

This all starts with you. You are the one who has to be committed to changing. If you are not one hundred percent dedicated to getting better, then you won't. You have to be willing to do whatever it takes to turn your life around. Whether this means attending therapy sessions or staying on medication, all of it is up to you. Health professionals can only do so much. They are not able to spend every second of the day by your side, giving you advice. In my case, I took everything I learned and applied it to my life. It's worked out pretty well for me.

Post-Traumatic Stress Disorder (PTSD)

My Post-Traumatic Stress Disorder has been categorized as complex and related to events that took place as a child. Most of the symptoms show up when I am either around women or when I am asleep.

I have a tough time in relationships with women. This is because they trigger flashbacks of how other women treated me when I was little. Through therapy I have worked in getting over this hump. I had to understand that not all women were like my mother. This is still a challenge to this day. Sometimes women around me will say or do things that remind me of my mother. I immediately get scared and try to keep them as far away as possible. I think it's a matter of self-preservation. I'll do anything in my power never to relive that pain again.

My other PTSD issues occur after eight o'clock at night. I think many of us do a majority of our thinking during the evening. We reflect; we ponder the future. Me? I tend to rehash my entire childhood every night.

In order to escape all of these bad thoughts, I take sleeping medication. These pills put me out of my misery and I can— eventually—fall asleep. The only trouble with falling asleep is the dreams that I have. I'll talk about them later on.

I rarely get a good night's sleep. I dread the evenings for this reason. That's why, in the past, I would drink myself to sleep. The alcohol was a depressant. It, along with the sleeping pills, would numb my brain so that I could get some rest.

Yes, I was using pills and booze. I was playing with fire when I put those two together. I woke up in the mornings in a complete daze. Somehow I'd make it through my classes and my job. I have no idea how I pulled it off. I was heavily drugged in class and still received some good grades. Looking back I am pretty proud—not about the drug addiction, but the good grades.

Dealing with PTSD

There are many symptoms of PTSD but I only suffer from a few: extremely bad dreams, feelings of guilt/worthlessness/depression, feeling emotionally numb, and difficulty sleeping. If you think you have any of the symptoms, do not immediately arrive at the conclusion that you have PTSD. I was diagnosed by more than one person. You may have another disorder entirely. But if you are told that you do have PTSD, I have some tips on how to get healthier.

1. Understand why you are having these flashbacks.

If you can identify the triggers then you will be able to understand the reasons behind the disorder. For me the triggers were certain events in my childhood that I had never really understood. I needed clarity about what took place and why. Once I was able to do this, my relationships with women slowly started to improve. I had longer relationships and more friends who were girls. I understood them better and realized that even if they acted like my mother at times, they would not treat me the same way. Sometimes I was wrong, and they did treat me like my mother had. So through these triumphs and failures I was able to see the women I was more compatible with, and what I wanted in a girlfriend. The gist of this is that identifying the source of the flashbacks helped me improve my life.

2. Write down all of your dreams.

This is a way you can find the source of your PTSD symptoms. I wrote down hundreds of dreams I had. Some people do not remember their dreams, but I always have. If you can recall them, definitely get them down on the page. When you get up, take a look at what you've written. See if you can find a constant symbol or pattern. If there is one there, focus on it. That aspect of your life is what is causing those awful dreams.

3. Learn from the dreams and flashbacks.

Take what you can from them. They'll shed light on the incidents that have made the greatest impact on you. I was able to gain a better understanding of my life by analyzing my flashbacks. Of course, I do recommend having a therapist to discuss these topics with. Having another set of eyes and ears never hurt anyone.

PTSD is one of the hardest things I have ever had to explain to anyone. Post-Traumatic Stress Disorder is the worst part of my life. I still suffer from it to this day. Some of my dreams caused by PTSD will haunt me 'til the day I die. I have noticed that the longer I have been away from my mom, the worse the dreams have become.

My bad dreams have been ongoing since I left my mother's house in 2010. I've woken up crying, sweating, and in a panic many times. Only those who suffer from the disorder can relate to how awful this can be. You relive the horrible events in your dreams. You can almost feel every emotion that you felt during the event. I'd like to share some of those experiences with you.

Dreams I have had:

• *Mom sitting in front of my crying her eyes out. She has cut her wrists and is blaming me for her suicide.* This one hurts the most. I have woken up screaming from this nightmare. It's absolutely terrifying; there's no other way to explain it. I can feel my mother's pain inside the dream. Her demented, tortured soul seeps into my mind. It's one of the most horrific things I have ever experienced.

• *Mom surrounded by all the girls I have dated. They are saying I am a failure and a fraud.* This one disturbs me. All these women, just yelling at me, is uncomfortable. However, I tend to be okay after waking up from these dreams.

• *My Dad dies and I have nobody to run to.* I am stuck with my abusive mother and her husband. Nobody believes what the two of them have done to me. I lock myself in my room and cry. There is no place to go.

The dreams were worse in the past, when I had a shot or two of whiskey before bed. The feelings of guilt, worthlessness and depression enveloped me at around 10 p.m. each night. I started to think about all of the people I had hurt, and sometimes I cried. I felt guilty for leaving my brothers at that house with my mom. I felt worthless because I'd been criticized for this choice so many times.

I am depressed because I have still not recovered from everything I went through. These thoughts, as you can guess, lead to trouble falling asleep. During the past several years I have tried taking many sleeping pills. Few of them have worked.

As I've gotten older I have become a night owl. I'll stay up till two or three in the morning, just thinking about my past. To be completely honest, I regret a great deal of my life. I have lied, cheated and done many other hurtful things to people. A great deal of that occurred before I entered therapy.

If I could have anything for Christmas, it would be a great night's sleep—one of those nights where you wake up and feel refreshed in the morning. I haven't experienced a night like that since I was a little boy.

That is what I wish for every night before I get into bed: a peaceful rest.

CHAPTER 29
Trying to Survive and Succeed:
Three Journal Entries

THE FOLLOWING JOURNAL ENTRIES DESCRIBE, IN GREATER detail, the thoughts going through my mind as I battled against anxiety, depression, and post-traumatic stress disorder. When I look back on these entries, I realize how far I've come and how much healthier I am today . . . and that I still have a long way to go.

December 2011

I have so many regrets, and I am only nineteen. My dreams revolve around the regrets. They haunt me on a daily basis. At times they are all I can think about. I cannot put the past behind me. The tragedies lie in the forefront of my mind. Most of them involve women I knew during high school. I squandered way too many opportunities. There were plenty of girls I could have had solid relationships with. They were beautiful girls who would have been great girlfriends with so much to offer. Instead I chose to play games and sabotage my relationships with them. I hurt them and myself in the process without even knowing it.

To be honest, this is because my self-esteem has been so low at certain points in my life. When your self-esteem is that low, you will go to any length to feel good. If that means dumping a girl to feel better about yourself, then you'll go ahead and dump her. At the time you may feel great about what you've done done. I felt like I was reborn every time I ended a relationship. I can't explain why. One has to be at that point to understand what I am talking about.

God, I hate myself though. If I could have just made some of the right choices! I always have taken the road less traveled. I think it suits me better. I like spending a lot of time alone. If someone gave me the choice of spending time with others or myself, I would choose the latter. I find it so peaceful, liberating and therapeutic to spend time alone. I learn more when I am with myself. I go to movies alone for this reason. I can watch the film and try to determine the writers' intentions, without any disruptions. I even enjoy being home alone for weeks at a time. All I do is create. I create art. I write poems, short stories, songs—anything I can think of. I bleed in front of the computer.

I wonder why I don't have many close friends. I think it's because I am so different from other people my age. I see the world differently than they do. Having essentially no childhood, going through so much adversity and bad luck, has hardened me. I am a forty-year-old in a twenty-year-old's body. I have often told close friends that I would be okay with dying now. That is how exhausted I am at times. Life can be so painful. When someone asks me about my life, three words come to mind: *dark, endless, grim.* I rarely see the bright side of things anymore. The bright side does not exist in my mind; only dark ominous clouds are in sight.

Just survive each day. If you wake up the next morning, then good for you. You must have done something right yesterday.

December 2011—further thoughts

I lost the ability to feel a few years ago. I have no idea where it went or even how it left me. All I know is that now I do not have the urge to fall in love or spend my life with somebody. Remember when you used to be that hopeless romantic? You would do anything for a girl that you were lusting over. Hell, you put every ounce of effort and time you had into that relationship. You put so much effort and time that you received the worst GPA of your academic career that year. That is how much you cared about that girl.

That idea seems secondary to me. I have so much to accomplish in such a short amount of time. Adding a person to my life would complicate things so much. I turn into an ugly person when I get into a relationship. I always wonder what the other person is doing and if she's going to dump me sooner or later. My self-esteem is so low in relationships that every day I wake up thinking the other person will break up with me. How sad is that?

Therefore, I end the relationship before I can get hurt. I usually do it by text message, and the girl and her friends hate my guts after that. I of course feel free and act like I it was bound to happen sooner or later.

In losing the ability to feel, I have found that I don't

really care about girls' feelings at all. I will hurt them with my words, even degrade them right in front of their faces. In a way it's like I don't even see them as people anymore. I see them as objects that can be manipulated so I can get what I want from them. This is because revealing who I truly am to anybody would be too painful.

I rely on accomplishments in order to have high self-esteem. I don't think I am a good person. I think it all started once I got into therapy. I started to "take what is mine" and not let anyone else have any. When "the good" comes my way I need to keep it to myself and not let it get away. I became more motivated than ever, but at the same time turned into more of an asshole. I think I need to go through this asshole stage in my life. It might be the only way I can eventually be a good husband and father.

Be honest, and be true to yourself. You are an aspiring young writer who will face some hardships, but in the end you will succeed. Nobody can stop you from achieving your dreams in this world. Your only bad trait is laziness, which you need to fight on an everyday basis. If you can topple that, then you can do anything you want to.

Put as much effort into your work and dreams as you did into that relationship with Nicole. Your new dream girl is a number-one best-selling book or a job as a sports writer. Put in the time and the effort and the results will come. Never let anyone outwork you and never let anybody tell you that you can't. You can. You always can. No matter how many times you fuck up.

You can achieve it all, Alex. You can reach for the stars and take them as your own. Take what is yours. Don't let anyone push you around or degrade you in any way. You mark your territory and defend your turf. You are a force to be reckoned with.

I think a lot of people are beginning to see that. I cannot be stopped. Nobody can break me down or end this thing. It is just too powerful and there are way too many emotions behind it.

February 2012

Depression sucks. I suffer from major depression and may never fully recover. But I can fight it as hard as I can. Depression is like a gigantic boulder placed on your body. No matter what you do, you can't get up. There is also nobody to help you through it. You're stuck.

The best way I can describe living through it is simple: imagine living every day in pain. Not actual physical pain, but the type of pain that breaks you down slowly. Each minute seems like an eternity. The pace of life slows down so much that you lose yourself in it. That is what happened to me during my junior and senior years at Bellarmine. I was living in a fog I could not escape. I had no energy and tried my best to survive.

Depression may be the most adversity I have ever faced in my life. This is because the type I have does not seem to go away. I have my good days, but I have far more bad days—days where my body seems to shut down. Getting up in the morning is as difficult as maxing out on the weight bench at the gym. Every action drains you. Paying attention is the hardest thing in the world. You just want to shut down.

I hate it. I really do. It prohibits me from putting all the effort I need to be successful in my life. I would trade anything in the world to escape depression. Some may ask, *Are you taking anything? Are you in therapy?* Yes, I am taking pills; and yes, I am in therapy. But both of those can only do so much. The rest I have to do on my own.

I believe it is a fight that's worth fighting. I have too many things I want to accomplish in my little amount of time here. I have started knocking down all the people who were in my way. Now I just have to push Depression, the five-million-pound boulder, off my back. He is always there—morning, afternoon, night—always wanting to bring me back down. He wants me to isolate myself so I can sulk in my sorrows. I can't let him do that. I have been fighting for too long. It is time to go in for the kill. All of this success has put him right where I want him. It's time to finish him off.

CHAPTER 30
Who Am I?

THESE ARE SOME OF THE MOST DIFFICULT WORDS I HAVE ever written. This is who I am. My name is Alex Fischler. As I write this I am twenty years old and still in college. Throughout the years I have learned a lot about myself. I am very private. I despise sharing personal details and sharing feelings even more. I am closed off, can be a shut in, and tend to isolate myself from the public when I can. I don't like taking credit for my accomplishments and still believe that I have much more to do. I hate the spotlight and will do whatever I can to stay away from it. I need to be this way. I *like* being this way. This is me.

Many people think that I am an asshole or that I'm weird. To those people, I do not care what you think. Anything you say or do to me is irrelevant. Once you've gone through hell and back, what others think about you does not matter. In my eyes, the only thing that matters is leaving no room for doubt in my life. In everything I do, this motto is present. I put all my effort into every aspect of my life. If I don't, there is no reason to live. Someone close to me once told me that I only have one shot at this "life thing." He said that I'd better take advantage of whatever comes my way. I wholeheartedly agree with him. So to all the doubters and haters, I don't care. Stop spending time hating me or trying to bring me down. It really is not worth it. I guarantee that you cannot touch me. There are too many people in your way to even try. After coming back from Los Angeles, I made sure this was the case. So stop, *now*. Move on with your life and start trying to make the world a better place. That is all I ask.

I have a gigantic hole in my heart. I have never had a true mother figure in my life. This has led to drinking, drugs, and many other bad addictions. I also have a difficult time trusting women. They have used me and tricked me way too many times.

***

Due to the guilt, depression and anxiety I rarely ever get to sleep before 3 a.m. I wake up every single morning in a great deal of pain, both physically and mentally. I am drained most of the time. I feel like a veteran who has just returned from war. At times during the day I have to stop to rest. Despite these hardships I try my best. I try to be the best person I can be with the amount of energy I am given each day. Sometimes I come up short, and that is unacceptable to me. Over the last few years I have come up short with many people. I apologize for that. None of this an excuse and I need to take responsibility for my behavior.

I truly am one of the most giving people out there. If you show me that I can trust you and you will not judge me; I will devote myself to being your friend. The truth is that I do not have many true friends. Most of the people I have associated with have either used me or played me. I will never understand why I am attracted to these kinds of people, but lately I have cut them out of my life. I want friends who are actually friends. People who care and want to spend time with me. This may sound like a call for help, but it is not. I am just stating my observations of myself. I do not want to be friends with most of the people my age. That is why I have a good amount of friends who are adults. They like me for who I am and are always willing to have fun. They do not judge me. They know all the pain and suffering I have been through. Instead of judging and criticizing, they try to help me grow. I love being around those who help me grow and change.

In terms of women, many also think I use girls and drop them. To be honest, I am pretty much one of the most hopeless romantics you will ever meet. Most of the material I write focuses on finding a girl who will like me for me. I will admit that I am not easy to be with. I have many flaws and struggle often. I long for a girl who I can enjoy life with and not have to prove anything to her. I already have to prove myself to so many others. When it comes to my personal life, I do not want to have to wow a girl. I do not see the need for that kind of nonsense. To be completely upfront, I want to give all my love to a girl for the first time. But I am afraid of getting hurt like so many others. First dates are difficult for me since girls immediately ask about family. I tell them I do not want to talk about that and usually there is no second date. People say that I should answer that question and see what happens. I have, and the result is the same. For once, I want to open up to a girl, and in return, have her understand instead of criticize me. I hope that one day I will find that girl. But if I do not, it will certainly not be the end of the world. I can do what I have done for many years now. Devote my time and efforts to my work.

Yes, I do want to have kids. If not with a woman, then I will adopt or find a surrogate. I would love to have three boys. I want to give my children the life I never had—a childhood without any worries in the world. That is the way it supposed to be. I want to teach them everything I know and help them grow into great men. That has always been a dream of mine.

Since I left my mother's house I have been trying to live the childhood that I never had. I spend my spare time on juvenile activities. I love listening to Disney and show tunes. I love going to Disneyland and other amusement parks. I eat Frosted Flakes and other kids' cereals for breakfast. I have been using the most recent years in an attempt to recreate a childhood. I must say it is one of the toughest tasks I have ever endeavored, especially since I am in college. Everyone is trying to grow up, while I'm trying to enjoy the little things that they no longer care about. This makes it difficult to make friends. But so be it. I have a lot of fun doing these activities on my own.

I devote four to six hours a day to studying art. By art I mean literature, film, music, and actual works of art. I want to touch on all of these during my lifetime, and I want to be great at them. The first step in the literature field was writing this book. In film I would love to write a few screenplays. Music wise I have plenty of songs written that I want to release down the road. I have also started using my body as a canvas. I now have a couple of tattoos and all of them represent important aspects of my life. They all mean something to me and I will never regret getting them. I think tattoos are a great way to show people what you value, what's important to you. I believe it is another art form. All art is extremely crucial to me. I learn so much when I spend time with a book or a film. Without those media, I feel like I may go insane.

For those whom I lied to, or deceived in the past, I am very sorry. Most of the lies I used to protect myself. That's how I survived in my household. This is not a justification for anything I said or did; it's just to give you some perspective.

Even though I don't deserve your forgiveness, I hope that you find it in your heart to forgive me.

Afterword
Thank You's and Apologies

I DECIDED TO WRITE LETTERS TO ALL OF MY FAMILY AND friends who have inspired me throughout my life. They deserve many thanks and praise. Others deserve apologies from me.

Dad

I do not know what to say to you. You know I how I feel about our relationship. You are my number-one supporter and have always given me everything I needed to survive. I apologize for all the times I made you look bad or disobeyed you. There was a point there where you had no control over me. I am sorry it ever had to be that way. There were too many times I disrespected you or talked back. You do not deserve that.

I want to say a few more things. You may not be the tallest or manliest of men I know. But your mental strength is unreal to me. You seem to be able to fight through anything and that trait has been passed on to me. You also have always set a great example. Whether it was never bad-mouthing my mother or preaching sportsmanship, I have learned so much from you.

The best part of our relationship in my mind is that we are also great friends. The crap we laugh about would be offensive to most people, but is the norm for us. Our love of sports has also played a major role in my life. Celebrating a huge win or a devastating loss, we have always had each other to console. I would not have it any other way. I want to thank you for all you have done. You have raised a good kid who has a lot to look forward to. You did your job, and now I'll do mine.

Love you Dad,

Alex

Uncle Peter and Uncle Mike

My uncles Peter and Mike have had my back since day one. Among many things they've done for me, Peter bought me my first nudie mag, and Mike got me an internship in Los Angeles. I cannot thank them enough. Both are incredibly supportive and will do anything to help me succeed.

Peter gave me the opportunity to humble myself through working on the construction crew for one of his real estate projects. I gained valuable experience doing the kind of work that many in this world have to do to get by. I met a few great men who were working their tails off to support their family.

After the two weeks of working construction, I realized how lucky I am to be in the position I am in. I also want to give my uncle a lot of credit. Despite the fact that he can be overbearing at times he has made a hell of a life for himself. He worked his ass off once he got to college and he was rewarded. So kudos to him. What I am even more proud of him for is the fact that he got married and adopted a child. I think these were gigantic steps for him and signs of growth. He is married to a wonderful woman and his new daughter is total cutie.

Mike allowed me to see what his life is like through an internship on one of the television shows he worked on.

I was given the privilege of seeing how professional television is made and understand the intricacies of the creative side. I even ended up being hired as an assistant writer for the last few weeks I was there. I really loved the people I worked with there and had a great time.

A letter to my grandma Bobbie

Dear Grandma,

I know you have your demons just like me. I am sorry for whatever happened to you that created the reality you live in today. I want to tell you that you did not deserve any of it. I hope one day you find peace. I love you and am always here for you. You have been a wonderful grandma to me and I appreciate all of your support throughout the years. I am also glad that you are living in a safer place. I was often worried about you at the house. I want the best for you and as a family we are going to make sure that happens. Please know that we all care about you. You are the matriarch of the Fischler family and we respect you for that.

Love always,

Your grandson Alex

Lucas Parelius

Dude,

You have been a great friend for the longest time. We started out as buds on our youth soccer team and our bond has been strong ever since. Between the two of us we have had our fair share of tragedies. The fact that you can relate to a majority of the crap I have gone though means so much to me. We see eye-to-eye on most issues and that is why our relationship is so great. To be honest, it really sucks that we do not go to school together anymore. You are one of the most outgoing guys I know and I enjoy being around you. You can lift my spirits and give me the energy to go have some fun. I want to thank you for being a true friend and always having my back. Know that I will always be there for you. I believe that we will be friends for the rest of our lives and I think you feel the same way.

Love you man,
Alex

Ryan Gleason

Ryan Gleason is one of my friends on the racquetball team at the University of Missouri. He is one of the most hilarious people I have ever encountered and is a selfless guy. I will always remember him screaming obscenities and porn lines on the racquetball court. I have rarely laughed harder than that in my life. We have had a pretty fun relationship and I look forward to another season of racquetball with him.

I want to thank him for accepting me and embracing me as a part of the team. He never made fun of me or anything like that, and I appreciate it.

The most important moment of our relationship occurred at Nationals this year in Arizona. We started talking about our pasts in the hallway of the hotel. I will not disclose any of the conversation, but I just want to let him know it meant a lot to me.

I love you bro,

Alex

Vanessa Vaughn

She could be the most naturally beautiful girl I know. I think many of my friends will agree with me. The beautiful dark blonde hair, blue eyes, and tanned skin could steal any man's heart. I am talking about Vanessa Vaughn, one of my closest female friends and confidantes.

I met Vanessa through Tommy Glasscott during the summer before my freshman year at Bellarmine. I remember talking to her for the first time; I was in awe from the start. She had to be the prettiest girl I had met in my life. No wonder Tommy had always talked about her. She was unreal.

At one point in time I tried to ask her out but that fizzled quickly. I was dealing with too much internally and at home so I was not in a normal state. I became too obsessed with the idea of her and that resulted in her backing off at a speed of 100 miles per hour, maybe even faster. I had no idea what I was doing and the consequences of my actions. For putting her through that I apologize and I believe we have both moved past that point.

As far as a friend goes, she is great. She is always there when I need her and warns me when it comes to women. I am vulnerable and easily manipulated once a girl starts to talk to me. Vanessa has given me some strength when it comes to that area of my life. She believes in me and she has no idea how important that is to me. I try to do the same for her when it comes to guys.

She has never fully comprehended how great of a girl she is. Her personality lights up a room and her sense of humor is perfect. She always understands my sarcasm and we get each other. I hope she knows that she deserves the world and nothing less. She works very hard and always tries to do the right thing. Any guy would be extremely lucky to spend time with her. I am not trying to put her on a pedestal or anything of that sort. She is really that amazing. I wish her the best and I hope we are always part of each other's lives.

I love you and more,
Alex

Nick Schmidt

Nick Schmidt is one of my close friends on the racquetball team at the University of Missouri. We have a great relationship mostly because we see eye-to-eye on most things, except sports. Kidding!

Nick and I had a stressful January trying to secure spots on the racquetball team. We were both confident we would make it, but in life nothing is certain. At the end of the week we found out we had both made it. I cannot tell you how ecstatic we were. I have never seen two guys be more relieved in my life.

I owe him a lot since he picked me up after a car accident in February. He also drove me to practices until I got my car back. In addition, he let me stay at his house during one of our tournaments. He is a very generous guy and has never asked for anything in return.

Nick and I bonded in the months leading up to Nationals. We talked about everything one could imagine. From sports, to girls, to even some philosophy every now and then. I remember one of the funniest conversations we had about fraternities and how we would never join one. Overall, Nick is a great guy and has a very bright future ahead of him. I look forward to another year of racquetball and all the laughs to come.

Love you bro,

Alex

Ally Miller

Ally is one of the most beautiful people I have ever met. Her long brown hair, brown eyes and sweet smile could steal any man's heart. She is not just a beautiful girl; she has a beautiful personality. To be completely honest, she is a joy to be around and I cannot express how wonderful she is. We have great conversations and make each other laugh quite often.

What makes our relationship so great is that fact that we get one another. We have been through similar experiences and have empathy for each other. A relationship like that can be hard to find, so I cherish what I have with her.

I will always remember the first day I met her in college.

I thought she was one of those selfish, superficial girls who doesn't care about anyone. Boy, was I wrong. She is very similar to me in this respect. She hides who she really is behind a few personas. It is an easy thing to do once you get the hang of it. Ally may appear to be superficial, but she is really one of the kindest people I know. She has a lot of love to give and people just need to give her the opportunity to show it.

During the last few weeks of the semester I had an urge to take a girl out. I asked Ally if she would want to go to a Rangers game with me. I think she said yes hesitantly because we hadn't talked all that much in class. On the subway ride over to Madison Square Garden I got to know a little bit about her. She was from Ohio, and in my eyes had a great family. We also had many things in common and shared similar interests. We both love sports, the arts, and working our asses off.

I didn't know this until I fully understood Ally, but she is one of the hardest working people I know. Her dream is to become a dancer in New York City and she will let nothing stand in her way. I truly admire her work ethic and the time and energy she dedicates to her craft.

To continue the story we had a great time at the Rangers

game. The conversation never seemed to die and the night went by very quickly. Christmas break was around the corner and I was ready to head home. Ironically enough Ally was in my psychology class during the spring semester. We talked every day in class, and in late April I sent her a text asking if she would want to go to a Yankees game with me. This time around there was no hesitation and she was excited to go.

I remember she wore a small Yankees jersey and tight jeans, along with some heels. She looked adorable. I gave her a Yankees sweatshirt in case she got cold and we were on our way. We arrived pretty close to first pitch and decided to grab some food at the concessions. The process of buying food with her may have been the funniest part of the night. We bickered like a married couple and she could not make up her mind on what she wanted to eat.

After that ordeal we sat down and enjoyed some baseball. It was a windy April night in New York and we left a little early. We hopped back on the train and headed back downtown. I remember her being so tired that she laughed at everything. I think the year had taken its toll on both of us and we were ready for summer. I ended up transferring to Missouri after the year ended, so I would not see Ally for a long time. We kept in touch over the summer and I started to confide in her often. Slowly she began to do the same—especially earlier this year when she went through one of the tougher stretches in her life. I think she began to trust me more after that rough patch.

In addition, she needs to know a few things about herself. She is braver than she will ever realize, she is special, and everything she wants is possible. All the hopes, dreams and goals she has can come true. If she ever needs any help I am here.

Alex

Brendan Giljum

Brendan Giljum is one of the nicest guys I have ever met. He is one of my good friends on the racquetball team at the University of Missouri. I really appreciate everything he has done for me since the first day I arrived on campus. He welcomed me on to the team with open arms and supported me throughout the year.

This guy unconditionally loves and supports his friends, which is a rare thing to find in the world. He also is a hell of a racquetball player and will have success in whatever he chooses to pursue.

I don't know anybody with more friends than Brendan.

The guy is so personable and easy to talk to—valuable skills to have in the world. Our relationship is one that I truly cherish. We have a lot of fun together on and off the court. I have hosted a few racquetball parties at my place and he always does something hilarious.

One of the fondest memories I will have of Brendan is he drank alcohol on the plane to Nationals. He got a very feminine drink and I found it hysterical.

I want to wrap this section up by again thanking Brendan for being Brendan. Without his hard work and kindness the racquetball team would not be what it is today.

Love you bro,

Alex

Taylor Roden

This guy is one of my closest friends. I don't have a lot of them, so that is saying something. I would consider him one of my confidantes and he is well-deserving. He has stayed with me through it all and I appreciate everything he has done for me.

Taylor has a big heart and really cares about others. When he likes a girl he commits to her. He is just one of those guys. Those are the types of guys that are hard to come by. Any girl would be lucky to have him. He will do anything for the people he loves.

He is one of the only people I still talk to from St. Martin of Tours. There is a reason for that. The first time we met was in first grade. He was new to our school and on the first day would not stop crying. I just laughed at him cause I didn't know what his problem was. He literally cried the whole day. But, we eventually became friends and it has been that way for a long time. We have had some great memories together.

One other reason I love Taylor so much is because he gets me. He understands why I make the decisions I make. He also understands what I have gone through. Whenever I have needed advice he is always there. Most of the time he leads me in the right direction. I could not have survived high school without his love and support. One of the best moments of our friendship has to be junior prom. He looked hilarious in his suit with his purple vest and shaggy hair. That night was pretty memorable. After the dance was over we headed back to my dad's place. He and his girlfriend Remi spent the night, along with another couple.

I know that he may have not approved of some of the shit I pulled in high school. That is why for a long period of time he didn't talk to me. I think we both grew during that time apart from one another and that has strengthened our friendship. Every time I'm in the Bay Area we either grab lunch or hang out.

We have similar values and that is especially evident when it comes to girls. He always has a new crush he wants to talk about with me. He sometimes even acts like a shy little girl about it. But I think it is hilarious and I love helping him. The guy has a very bright future as well. He is incredibly smart and works his butt off. He is going to a great school so he is doing all the right things. I wish him the best of luck in the future and hope we will be lifelong friends.

My brother, Zachary Fischler

Zachary, I love you more than you will ever know. I am so lucky to have you as my brother. You are one of the kindest and most generous people I know. You try your best given the cards you were dealt. You are a great brother and I hope you know that. I think about you and Max every day I am away from home.

I am sorry that you may not understand some of the decisions I have made in my life. Leaving home had nothing to do with you. I am happy that you love your mom and have a great relationship with her. You deserve that. I am also sorry for any of the harsh things I have said to you in the past.

I want you to succeed so badly. You are so smart and have many unique gifts that you will be able to share with the world. I love talking with you about anything and never hesitate to call me whenever. Despite the fact I have distanced myself from the family, I will never distance myself from you. You and Max mean the world to me. You are blood and we have been through too much together to throw it away. I know we have our disagreements and rarely see eye to eye. But in the grand scheme of things we are brothers.

I know you will be great at whatever you do. Don't worry about what everyone has to say. Just be you and that is okay. If people do not like you for who you are, then that is their problem.

Love you,

Alex

My brother, Maxwell Fischler

Maxwell, I love you so much. I have seen you grow from a little infant all the way into the teenager you are today. We have had our ups and downs, but overall you are a great brother. I know I may criticize you at times, but as I said to Zachary as well, I just want you to be the best you can be. This applies to everything you do in life, whether that is playing hockey or your schoolwork.

I want you to also know that none of the decisions I have made in my life have anything to do with you. I know when I first left you were pretty distraught about it. But I think as time goes on you will understand why I left. I had to think about what was best for me at that point in my life. A time will come when you have to make difficult decisions that others will not agree with. You just need to trust your gut and everything will turn out fine.

The biggest piece of advice I can give you is this: Do not live your life based on what others think of you. I know that this might be tough to understand in high school. But in the long run, you need to be *you*. Don't imitate me or mold yourself into what someone wants you to be. Just be yourself and that is more than enough.

Love you,

Alex

Steven Karr

My best friend—I love you man. I don't think you will ever realize how much you mean to me. You are one of the only people I can trust in this world. You understand who I am and why I make certain lifestyle choices. You know what I want to be and what I have to do to attain that goal. You respect me and you rarely ever criticize me. You are also one hundred percent behind me in everything I do. I could not ask for a better friend.

I can only hope to be as great a friend as you have been to me. Whenever I need you, you are there. No matter how rough it has gotten you always have my back. To vomiting my guts out when I first started taking anti-depressants, to standing up for me in high school, you are my guy. I hope that you understand how appreciative I am. I am so lucky to have you in my life.

Your family has also embraced me as well. We have also had some great times together. Whether it was spending New Year's together throwing chocolate pretzels on girls' porches to sitting in Mathurin's stats class, it has been a blast. I know that we will probably be best buds forever and that is what I want. There is nobody else in the world I would rather call my best friend than you. I do not think I could have made it through high school without you. Hell, we still talk pretty much every day and always want to know what is going on in the other's life. I enjoy every moment of it.

I think you are going to be a great director and have a great future ahead of you.

Love you,

Alex

Tommy Glasscott

Tommy, I had a rough time writing this. I didn't know how to express how I feel about you. We have been through so much together and practically known each other since kindergarten. I cannot explain how much our relationship means to me. We have had many ups and downs, but we always seem to find a middle ground. Once we get to that middle ground, things seem to be great.

You have taught me a lot in this life. Especially when it comes to friends. Your real friends are the ones that are always there. Despite the fact that others may criticize you for having me as a friend, your loyalty has rarely ever wavered. I love you for this and because you are one of the funniest people I know. Making up songs and dances with you has been a pleasure. Even sleeping in the same bed with you has had its moments. I have never literally been closer to another guy in my life. Ha ha. We have gotten hammered together and have battled over getting a girl.

I apologize for any times I have hurt you or not been the friend you wanted. My last intention was to hurt you or make you think I was not loyal. I wish you the best in the future and hope we will always remain close friends.

Love,

Alex

Matt Weingarten

Matt is one of the most caring and understanding individuals I know. He probably knows me better than many of my family members do. That is how close we have become over the years. For a long time we knew each other, but never became friends. Our relationship really started in chemistry class during our junior year. We sat next to one another and I essentially shared all my problems with him. He took it all in stride and attempted to give his best advice to me.

Little did I know, he was going through similar difficulties in his own life. That is why he understood me so well. I think our similar backgrounds are what make our relationship so great. We have spent nights just discussing our perceptions of the world. We both find each other's opinions so fascinating. Boy, some of the talks we have had. They range from why we are here to why girls are the way they are. I want to thank Matt for always being there.

He has always had my back whenever I have needed it. It is an honor to call him one of my best friends. I hope that we are this tight for the rest of our lives. I always need someone to talk philosophy with. I wish him the best of luck at Seattle U and anything else he pursues in the rest of his life. He definitely has the passion and the work ethic to make any dream a reality.

Love you buddy,
Alex

Brenda Lee

Brenda, you are my surrogate Mom. I know that when you first met me you didn't have a ton of experience around kids. But, I want to let you know that you have done a tremendous job. You care about me, love me, and always are looking out for my best interests. What else could I ask for in a step mom?

The most important thing you have given me is unconditional love. No matter what you have seen me say or do, you have loved me. I want to thank you for everything. I hope that you are always a part of our family. I cannot imagine any more holidays without you. You are the mother I have always wanted and you understand me so well. I do not think you realize how much that means to me. I also appreciate all the girl advice you have given to me. It has definitely changed my perspective on the dating world.

I also want to say that I love you so much. I love your personality and how caring you are. You are the most selfless woman I have ever met. The fact that you have stayed by my father's side over the last few years amazes me. Many women would have bolted as quickly as possible. You on the other hand embraced the challenge and have been nothing but supportive of him. I can only hope I find a wife as good as my Dad has found in you. I am excited for the wedding next May and cannot wait for you to officially be a part of our family. It has been a long time coming.

I love you Brenda,

Alex

Barbara and Larry Caskey

You two are the best grandparents I could ask for. Since I was a little boy you have done everything for me. I remember the days when all I wanted to do was go up to your house and spend time with both of you. Those were my best childhood memories. You have been at every one of my games, VIP days in grade school and every other event. You have supported me through thick and thin.

I am sorry for some of the decisions I have made in the past. Please know that none of them have to do with you. Also, there is nothing you could have done to prevent the horrible things that took place. None of what my mother did is a reflection on you two. She is her own person who made her own decisions. You both did your best and that is all I can ask.

I am happy that we have a pretty good relationship at the moment. I believe both of you have made the right choice in moving away from San Jose. There is too much drama there and you needed to remove yourself from it all. Try to enjoy each other as much you can. Since you are both retired you should have plenty of time to do that. In addition, try to not to worry about me. I am doing as well as I ever have and will continue to flourish. I wish you guys the best in the future.

Love,

Alex

Rebecca Janicki

You have always been a great aunt to me. I want to thank you for all you have done. I know for a long time we were not that close. But since I moved out you have been there for me. I remember the long phone conversation we had when I was living back in New York. I told you everything that had happened and you began to cry. You apologized for the abuse and said you wished I had told you. But you knew I could never have really told you. That would have brought you into the mess I was dealing with for so many years.

I want to commend you on the type of mother you are to your children. You are running a great family down in San Diego; your kids are happy and healthy. Also, do not worry about the scar across my nose. That was not your fault. The scar defines who I am. All the new people I meet ask me about it. I get to tell different stories all the time about what exactly happened. Not once have I put the blame on you. Again, thanks for being there and understanding all of my pain.

Love and more,

Alex

David Faron

I am lucky that you found me on a housing Web site. You will never have any idea how fortunate I was to get you and Alex as roommates. Even though you guys gave me a lot of shit, I couldn't care less.

The most important thing is that I enjoyed living with you two. You helped me feel at home and that was crucial. I cannot thank you enough for your support over the last year. You were a great roommate, friend and taught me so much. We had some great nights and you introduced me to the real college life.

I also appreciate you welcoming me into the Faron family. Not many people do that, so I value the relationships I have with you guys. I will never forget some of the laughs and some of the arguments. I look back on those hockey discussions with a smile. I got to see your point of view of the game, which is now another perspective I can use going forward.

I hope you figure you out what your plans are sooner rather than later. You have a tremendous work ethic and will be successful at whatever you decide to do. Just try to stay on the right side of the law and avoid fights. You only get so many screw-ups in this life 'til one permanently grounds you. I wish you the best of luck in the future and hope we remain friends despite the geographical distance that will separate us.

Love you man,

Al

Alex Killian

You, my friend, are one of the most interesting guys I know. I mean that in a good way. You have no problem spending a whole day in your room and never seeing the light of day. I guess years of playing XBox can do that to you.

Here I want to say how much I appreciate you. I had a great time with you over the last eight months. I will cherish every Friday night we had. When you are under the influence of alcohol you are hysterical. From lighting David's arm on fire to telling every girl in the bar to talk to me 'cause I was from California, you are never boring.

You also gave me many nicknames that nobody else will ever call me. From Allantown to Zander, it all made me laugh. I appreciate your kindness and all the times you helped me during the year. I could not have made it to this point without you.

I wish you the best of luck in your journey to becoming a

dentist. I think you are an incredibly bright guy with a great future ahead of you. Just put in the work and do what you do, man. You know what it is going to take; make it happen. Like I said in David's letter, I hope we remain friends well into the future. The relationship we have means a lot to me and I think you are a great friend. Keep in touch and come out to Cali anytime.

Love you man,

Al

Gene Pare

I consider you to be a surrogate father to me in many ways. I cannot thank you enough for the time and efforts you have put into my racquetball career. I remember the first racquetball lesson I had with you. All I did was hit what seemed like million backhand shots for an hour. I got home that day and my whole right side was sore.

You developed me into the player I am today and it shows. You have always been there to support me, and I appreciate it. We have a lot in common and can talk about things other than racquetball. You are an inspiration to me and I am a better person because of you. Whether I am playing racquetball or dealing with others I always think to myself,

What would Gene do? Ninety-nine percent of the time that is the right choice to make. You truly have set a great example for me and I live my life by it. You treat others with respect and kindness, which is rare in this world. I have never met someone who exemplifies how an athlete should act. I know that you have reached great heights in racquetball and are still one of the most humble people out there. I hope we continue to have a great relationship into the future. I still need to develop my game a little more and I look forward to putting more work in with you on the court.

Love and more,

Alex

Bud Geracie

One of the most influential people in my life. When I look at you I see myself in thirty years. I am proud to say I consider you a surrogate father. We have so much in common that it scares me at times. There have been conversations where we literally say the same thing at the same time. That is how much on the same page we are.

You understand me better than most of the people in my own family. You get the way I feel and why I feel that way. The fact that you have gone through some of the same hardships has made a huge impact on me. Without your love and support I guarantee there is no way I would be alive today. All of those late-night dinners, venting sessions and everything else have been amazing.

We also have had several dimensions in our relationship. From coach to player, friend to friend, mentor to student and boss to employee. All of them have been fun and learning experiences for me. You have given me the wisdom to understand that maybe, just maybe, my life will turn out okay. Every time I have a doubt you are there to suppress it. I also appreciate every single piece of advice you have given me. I use it in my everyday life, especially when my dark clouds come. I know I will be able to pull through because of you. I hope that our relationship remains the same for the rest of my life. I value every conversation and moment we have together.

Love and thanks,

Alex

***

Finally, I want to thank Bellarmine College Prep for all their help. Throughout my high school career their counseling department, faculty and other students were behind me one hundred percent. My therapists at that school went above and beyond to make sure my life stayed in place throughout all the traumatic events. They played a huge role in my recovery and I owe them more in then they will ever know.

I do not believe that I would have received the same treatment at any other high school. The teachers at this school inspired me to be a writer. Bill Healy, Jim Harville and Tom Alessandri were all instrumental in my writing career.

People need to know what a tremendous institution Bellarmine is. There is no place like it in the world. The bonds I made at that school will never be broken. I also met my best friend there. We were just sitting in a sophomore English class and started talking sports. We have been inseparable ever since.

Those are the type of friendships I made there. The brotherhood is something that I will cherish forever. I will always remember the football games, rallies, assemblies and laughs in class. Bellarmine's motto is "men for others." I try to embody that slogan everyday of my life. The lessons I learned at this school shaped who I am today. I am proud to say that I am a Bell Alum. The impact this school had on me is tremendous and I have nothing but praise for the community.

Love and more,

Alex

About the Author

ALEX FISCHLER was born in Santa Clara, California, and raised in nearby San Jose. He has written for the *Columbia* (Mo.) *Daily Tribune*, the sports department of the *San Jose* (Calif.) *Mercury News*, and has freelanced for other publications. An All-American racquetball player, Alex was a California state champion as a teenager and recently competed in the Wilson International Collegiate Championships in Tempe, Arizona. A graduate of the prestigious Bellarmine College Preparatory School, Alex is currently studying English and Film at the University of Missouri in Columbia, Missouri. You can reach him at af253@mail.missouri.edu or via the publisher at duffincreative.com.